SPECIAL REPORTS

THE KILLING OF
GEORGE FLOYD

BY DUCHESS HARRIS, JD, PhD, WITH ALEXIS BURLING

Essential Library

An Imprint of Abdo Publishing | abdobooks.com

abdobooks.com

Published by Abdo Publishing, a division of ABDO, PO Box 398166, Minneapolis, Minnesota 55439. Copyright © 2021 by Abdo Consulting Group, Inc. International copyrights reserved in all countries. No part of this book may be reproduced in any form without written permission from the publisher. Essential Library™ is a trademark and logo of Abdo Publishing.

Printed in the United States of America, North Mankato, Minnesota.
102020
012021

Cover Photo: Zach D Roberts/NurPhoto/Getty Images
Interior Photos: Alessandro Bremec/NurPhoto/AP Images, 4–5; Alex Milan Tracy/Sipa USA/Newscom, 9; Shutterstock Images, 12–13, 76–77, 79, 89, 97; Eric Gay/AP Images, 14–15; Art Wager/iStockphoto, 18; Stephanie Kenner/Shutterstock Images, 21; iStockphoto, 24–25, 29; Keystone-France/Gamma-Keystone/Getty Images, 34; Chester Brown/Alamy, 36; Julio Cortez/AP Images, 38–39, 59; Bebeto Matthews/AP Images, 44, 62–63; John Minchillo/AP Images, 47, 61, 90–91; Jeff Baenen/AP Images, 49; Stephen B. Morton/AP Images, 50–51; Jose Luis Magana/AP Images, 52–53; Richard Tsong-Taatarii/AP Images, 55; Martial Trezzini/AP Images, 64–65; Javier Pina/Shutterstock Images, 68; Virginia Mayo/AP Images, 73; Michal Urbanek/Shutterstock Images, 74–75; Jerry Holt/Star Tribune/Getty Images, 84; Nick Wass/AP Images, 95; David Brickner/Shutterstock Images, 99

Editor: Alyssa Krekelberg
Series Designer: Maggie Villaume

Library of Congress Control Number: 2020942381

Publisher's Cataloging-in-Publication Data

Names: Harris, Duchess, author. | Burling, Alexis, author.
Title: The killing of George Floyd / by Duchess Harris and Alexis Burling
Description: Minneapolis, Minnesota : Abdo Publishing, 2021 | Series: Special reports | Includes online resources and index
Identifiers: ISBN 9781532194610 (lib. bdg.) | ISBN 9781098214067 (ebook)
Subjects: LCSH: Police shootings--Juvenile literature. | Police brutality--United States--Juvenile literature. | Excessive force used by police--Juvenile literature. | Race relations--Juvenile literature.
Classification: DDC 363.232--dc23

CONTENTS

Chapter One
"I CAN'T BREATHE"   4

Chapter Two
WHO WAS GEORGE FLOYD?   14

Chapter Three
THE HISTORY OF POLICE BRUTALITY   24

Chapter Four
PROTESTS AND RIOTS IN MINNEAPOLIS   38

Chapter Five
A NATION DIVIDED   52

Chapter Six
GLOBAL SUPPORT   64

Chapter Seven
A CALL FOR REFORM   76

Chapter Eight
GEORGE FLOYD'S LEGACY   90

Essential Facts   100   Source Notes   106
Glossary   102   Index   110
Additional Resources   104   About the Authors   112

"I CAN'T BREATHE"

I t was a sweltering evening, around eight o'clock on Monday, May 25, 2020, when four police officers—Derek Chauvin, Tou Thao, J. Alexander Kueng, and Thomas Lane—got a call over their radios. According to a clerk at Cup Foods, a convenience store in Minneapolis, Minnesota, a customer had just used a counterfeit $20 bill to buy cigarettes. When confronted about the fake money, the customer, who the clerk said seemed "awfully drunk" and "not in control of himself," refused to hand over his purchase.[1]

A few minutes later, Kueng and Lane arrived at the scene. They saw a Black man in a dark-colored tank top who fit the clerk's description. He was sitting in a blue

The words *I can't breathe* became a rallying cry after George Floyd's death.

SUV parked across the street from the store. They walked over to the car.

"Hands on top of your head. Step out of the vehicle and step away from me, alright?" Lane, who is white, said, drawing his gun.

"Okay, Mr. Officer, please don't shoot me," replied 46-year-old George Floyd, who sat behind the wheel. "Please man."

"Step out and face away. I'm not shooting," said Lane, holstering his gun.[2]

Floyd kept talking but didn't budge. So Lane grabbed Floyd's arm and pulled him out of the vehicle.

"I'LL DO ANYTHING. I'LL DO ANYTHING Y'ALL TELL ME TO, MAN. I'M NOT RESISTING. I'M NOT! I'M NOT!"[3]

—GEORGE FLOYD TO POLICE

He handcuffed Floyd's hands behind his back, then Kueng walked Floyd to a nearby wall. According to the official transcript of the event, Lane and Kueng attempted to arrest Floyd for using a fake bill. When they tried to get Floyd into the police car, he refused to go inside, saying that he was claustrophobic.

Nine minutes into the arrest, another squad car arrived carrying officers Thao and Chauvin. Both had prior complaints filed against them for the use of excessive force. Chauvin, the senior member in the group, tried to get Floyd into the police vehicle. For unknown reasons, he then went around to the other side and pulled Floyd through the squad car and onto the pavement.

While Floyd was facedown on the blacktop, Lane, Kueng, and Chauvin pressed against Floyd's body, with Chauvin kneeling on his neck. Witnesses started filming the encounter on their smartphones. At 8:20 p.m., Floyd's voice can be heard clearly on one of the recordings.

"I can't breathe, man. Please," he said.[4]

The officers radioed in a Code 2 to dispatch, the signal used for nonemergency medical assistance, because

Floyd was bleeding from the mouth. A minute later, they upgraded the call to a Code 3, signifying a medical emergency, because Floyd kept saying he couldn't breathe and the officers wondered whether he was under the influence of substances.

By this point, a crowd had gathered due to all the commotion. A little after 8:20 p.m., 17-year-old witness Darnella Frazier started filming. Her close-up footage shows Chauvin's knee lodged into Floyd's neck.

"I can't believe this, man," Floyd gasped. "Mom, I love you. Tell my kids I love them. I'm dead."[6]

Chauvin kept his knee in place. In total, he held the position for around eight minutes. In that time, Floyd said

Protesters held up Floyd's picture on May 29, 2020, both to remember him and to seek justice for his death.

"I can't breathe" more than a dozen times. At 8:25 p.m., he appeared to be unconscious.

Meanwhile, bystanders at the scene shouted for the police to stop. They begged Chauvin to take his knee off Floyd's neck, but Chauvin did not. When the ambulance appeared at 8:27 p.m., the paramedics confirmed that Floyd didn't have a pulse.

"YOU JUST REALLY KILLED THAT MAN, BRO. YOU JUST REALLY KILLED THAT MAN."[8]

—BYSTANDER AT THE SCENE

Chauvin kept his knee on the unresponsive man's neck for another minute and 20 seconds, until the emergency medical technicians told him to get up. They loaded Floyd onto a stretcher, and the ambulance left the scene. At 9:25 p.m., Floyd was pronounced dead at a nearby hospital.

CHOKE HOLD

Because of its ability to permanently cripple the spine or cut off the airways of a victim, the choke hold is no longer taught during training at many police departments in the United States. In those where it's still allowed, the move is only supposed to be used when an officer feels like his or her life is in danger. But because it's difficult to prove whether an officer's life is on the line in a particular instance, many people argue choke holds and neck restraints should not be allowed at all because of the damage they can inflict.

In 2012, there were 79 reported instances of this restraint technique being used in Minneapolis, according to police department records. The number dropped to 40 in 2018 but rose again to 56 in 2019.[9] Calls to prohibit these potentially lethal restraints altogether have gotten louder since Floyd's death.

POLICE INFRACTIONS

The New York Times contacted experts who noted that applying force to the neck while Floyd was lying facedown on the ground compressed his chest. This blocked the flow of oxygen to his lungs. Additionally, the choke hold Chauvin was using is only allowed in Minneapolis when a suspect is actively resisting arrest. But Floyd wasn't resisting at that point.

Critics also said the four officers weren't sufficiently clear when reporting the seriousness of Floyd's medical condition. They didn't provide any medical treatment to Floyd while waiting for the ambulance to arrive. By the time the paramedics got Floyd into the ambulance, he had gone into cardiac arrest.

Autopsies done by the Hennepin County medical examiner and Floyd's family ruled his death a homicide.[10] But Chauvin's defense attorney says Floyd died from a drug overdose. An autopsy revealed that Floyd had methamphetamine and fentanyl, two dangerous illegal drugs, in his system. Despite the debate about what killed Floyd, his death sent shock waves through Minneapolis. It would also spark a movement that would spread across the country and around the world.

CAPTURING POLICE BRUTALITY ON FILM

Cell phone videos posted to social media help spread the word when police brutality occurs. But filming such an event can take a toll on the person taking the video. On May 25, 2020, Darnella Frazier was taking her nine-year-old cousin to Cup Foods when she saw police officers forcefully detaining Floyd. She took out her phone and recorded the scene. After it was over, Frazier posted the video on Facebook. The next day, the four cops involved in Floyd's death were fired.

Frazier was traumatized by what she had witnessed. She was also criticized online for not doing more to de-escalate the situation. But Frazier says she did what she could. "If it wasn't for me, four cops would've still had their jobs, causing other problems. My video went worldwide for everyone to see and know," she said.[11]

FROM THE HEADLINES

THREE WORDS, 70 CASES

The *New York Times* studied police records and found that in the decade before Floyd's death, at least 70 people had died in police custody after saying "I can't breathe." More than half of these people were Black, including in the cases below.[12]

Byron Williams was pulled over in 2019 in Las Vegas, Nevada, because his bike didn't have a light. He initially tried to ride away, but he stopped and complied with the officers' orders. Still, they pinned him facedown in the dirt. He said "I can't breathe" 17 times before he fell unconscious and died.[13]

In 2014 near Glendale, Arizona, police officers went to a couple's home after reports of an argument. When they arrived, Balantine Mbegbu and his wife said everything was fine. But the cops pushed Mbegbu to the floor, punched him in the head, tased him, and shoved their knees into his neck. After foaming from the mouth and vomiting, he died while his wife was watching.

One high-profile case occurred in 2014 in New York City. Police officer Daniel Pantaleo arrested Eric Garner for selling untaxed cigarettes on the street. Despite Garner's pleas for air, Pantaleo put him in a choke hold that eventually killed him, a maneuver banned by the New York Police Department since 1993. After five

A Center for Policing Equity report noted that in the United States, police are more likely to use aggressive tactics on Black people than they are on white people.

years and two criminal investigations, only two of more than a dozen officers involved in the Garner case faced disciplinary action. Sergeant Kizzy Adonis took a plea to give up 20 vacation days and kept her job. Officer Pantaleo was fired in August 2019. He filed a lawsuit two months later, trying to get his job back.

CHAPTER TWO

WHO WAS GEORGE FLOYD?

O
n the last day of George Floyd's junior year at Jack Yates High School in Houston, Texas, he and a few close friends were walking home, celebrating the start of summer. They discussed what they hoped might happen when they finally became seniors. One friend whom George had met on the first day of sixth grade, 17-year-old Jonathan Veal, asked the others what they wanted to do with their lives. "George turned to me and said, 'I want to touch the world,'" said Jonathan.[1]

Jack Yates High School alumni gathered for a candlelight vigil to remember Floyd on June 8, 2020.

GROWING UP IN THE BRICKS

George was born in Fayetteville, North Carolina, on October 14, 1973. Soon after, his parents, Larcenia Floyd and George Perry, got divorced. When he was two, his mother relocated the family to the Third Ward in Houston to find more job opportunities. They moved into a public housing complex south of downtown called the Cuney Homes. Directly across the street from Texas Southern University, the massive group of buildings was often referred to by the community as "the Bricks."[2] Throughout his childhood, George and his four younger siblings made do with what little they had. Larcenia worked at a fast-food restaurant. But the family rarely had much money.

George didn't get good grades, but he excelled in sports, especially basketball and football. He was an imposing force on the Jack Yates High School football team as a tight end. In 1992, he led his team to the state championship. And Floyd's talent on the basketball court

16

caught the eye of a college basketball coach.

After graduating from high school in 1993, George enrolled in South Florida Community College, now South Florida State College, on a basketball scholarship. He became the first member of his family to attend college. But living in Florida didn't suit him, and he missed his family. He transferred to Texas A&M's Kingsville campus in 1995. Two years into that experience, he left school early without getting his degree.

A CHANGING THIRD WARD

Not long after Houston was founded in 1836, the Third Ward cropped up as a subdivision located southeast of downtown. In the early 1900s, the area's population was evenly divided between Black and white residents. But by the 1930s, more Black people had moved in, and the area became known as a haven for art and culture. Today it is home to various museums and the Black Ensemble Theatre. The oldest Black church as well as the only Black-owned bank in the state are also located in the Third Ward.

But as is the case in many poor neighborhoods within cities, the Third Ward has been slowly gentrifying since the early 2000s. Wealthy people, most of them white, started moving in. It was once a low-income area with public housing projects. Now luxury townhomes have cropped up on the west side.

TROUBLE IN HOUSTON

In 1997, Floyd returned home to Houston, where he worked in construction and security. He also developed a reputation for playing music and rapping. His deep

Houston is one of the most populated cities in the United States, with more than 2.3 million people living there.

baritone voice appeared on mixtapes created by DJ Screw, a fixture in Houston's hip-hop scene in the 1990s.

Like many people his age in the area, Floyd also got mixed up with drugs. Throughout his twenties, Floyd was arrested for a number of drug-related crimes, according to court and police records. In one incident in 2004, he was arrested for a ten-dollar drug deal and spent ten months in jail. Then in 2009, he was sentenced to five years in prison for a burglary he'd committed two years prior. He and five other men had broken into a woman's apartment, according to official records. Floyd was the one who had held the gun and threatened the homeowner. He pleaded guilty to aggravated robbery with a deadly weapon.

A CHANGED MAN

When 39-year-old Floyd returned home from prison in 2013, he decided it was time to turn his life around. He started advising kids in his neighborhood to stay away from violence. "I've got my shortcomings and my flaws," Floyd once said in a video that he posted to social media. "But, man, the shootings that's going on, I don't care what 'hood you're from . . . put them guns down."[4] He volunteered for Resurrection Houston, a local church. He also got involved with a local

"[FLOYD] HAD MADE SOME MISTAKES THAT COST HIM SOME YEARS OF HIS LIFE. AND WHEN HE GOT OUT OF THAT, I THINK THE LORD GREATLY IMPACTED HIS HEART."[6]

—RONNIE LILLARD, A FRIEND OF FLOYD'S

religious organization that moved men to Minnesota for drug-rehabilitation and job-placement services. Floyd liked the idea of a fresh start so much that he decided to relocate to Minnesota as well in 2014.

Floyd's years in Minnesota were fruitful and productive. He moved into a duplex in Saint Louis Park, a suburb of Minneapolis. In 2017, he got a job as a security guard. After a year, with the help of his landlord who owned a dance club, he became a bouncer at the Conga Latin Bistro in Minneapolis. He had multiple kids from previous relationships, and in 2017 he started dating Courtney Ross, a manager at a local coffee shop. "He [was] such a spiritual man beyond just being prayerful and a man of God," Ross said about

DIFFICULTIES AFTER PRISON

According to the Department of Justice, more than half a million inmates are released from prison every year. Although getting out of jail means more freedom, the transition can be difficult. One of the most common challenges is finding suitable housing with a landlord who will rent to ex-convicts.

Many former inmates also have trouble finding jobs. Though many states have laws that prevent employers from asking about criminal records on job applications, employers can still do background checks later in the hiring process. According to the National Institute of Justice, Black applicants with criminal records are turned down for jobs nearly twice as often as white applicants with criminal records.[7]

Floyd. "He had a sense about him that just made you feel comforted, feel good, feel validated."[8]

A LIFE CUT SHORT

Beginning in 2018, Floyd went through some difficult times. His mother died that year. Then in February 2020, the COVID-19 pandemic hit the United States. Floyd came down with the virus but recovered. Then he was laid off

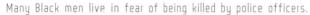
Many Black men live in fear of being killed by police officers.

MORE TO THE
STORY

THE CORONAVIRUS PANDEMIC

Coronaviruses typically lead to upper respiratory illnesses, including the common cold. At the end of 2019, scientists detected a new, dangerous type of coronavirus. Called SARS-CoV-2, it first appeared in Wuhan, China, and caused the disease named COVID-19. In early 2020, the virus spread throughout the region and then the world. Doctors reported cases of people suffering from pneumonia-like symptoms. Most who got the disease recovered, but a lot of people died.

Because of the seriousness of the disease and the speed at which it spread, the World Health Organization declared the situation a pandemic in March 2020. In September of that year, COVID-19 had spread to more than 170 countries. More than 33 million people worldwide had fallen ill. At least one million people had died.[9]

Federal, state, and local governments took extreme measures to combat the spread of the disease at the start of the pandemic. They ordered the immediate closure of restaurants, bars, shopping malls, and stores. Events both large and small were canceled. Schools stopped all in-person classes, and students started taking classes online. People were ordered to stay home and not leave except for necessary outings. Due to the shutdown, many businesses suffered and people lost their jobs. Floyd was one of many people who were laid off because of the pandemic.

from his job along with other employees when the state issued a mandatory stay-at-home order, causing many restaurants and bars to close.

Floyd was committed to spending time with his partner and friends after he recovered from COVID-19. In the days following Floyd's death, many of his friends and family members expressed their horror about what had happened to him. Floyd isn't the first Black man to die at the hands of the police. In fact, throughout many decades in the United States, thousands of people have been victims in similar circumstances. To understand the fight against police brutality on the streets today, it's important to look back at the movement throughout history.

CHAPTER THREE

THE HISTORY OF
POLICE
BRUTALITY

I n a 2020 exhibit at the Smithsonian's National
Museum of African American History and Culture,
a cardboard sign hangs on the wall. Red and white
letters stand out against a yellowing background. "We
demand an end to police brutality *NOW!*" is printed on
the front.[1] But the placard isn't something that was used
in protests after Floyd's death. It was first held high by a
civil rights protester during the March on Washington in
1963, which was led by, among others, Dr. Martin Luther
King Jr.

The National Museum of African American History and Culture has
many exhibits. Some have focused on slavery and others on the civil
rights movement.

"This idea of police brutality was very much on people's minds in 1963, following the years, decades really, of police abuse of power and then centuries of oppression of African Americans," says William Pretzer, the senior history curator at the museum.[2] During the civil rights movement in the mid-1950s and 1960s, people took to the streets to protest racial inequality. They held signs, shouted slogans, and spoke out against what they saw as a long history of prejudice, violence, and murder at the hands of law enforcement.

Americans of various races and ethnicities have been subjected to police brutality throughout history. For example, in the 1920s, Italian immigrants were targeted by police because of their perceived connections to the Mafia, an organized crime group from Italy. During the decade following the September 11, 2001, terrorist attacks in New York City and Washington, DC, many Muslim Americans were harassed by police because of their perceived connections to terrorism. But according to University of Texas at Austin history professor Leonard Moore, the majority of police-on-citizen violence throughout US history has been against Black people.

THE ROOTS OF MODERN POLICING

What people think of today as the police department didn't arise until the late 1830s. Before that time, in the 1600s and 1700s, people from the community volunteered to serve as night watchmen. They were responsible for cracking down on illegal activities such as prostitution and gambling.

When communities grew too large to be monitored by volunteer forces, cities created official organizations. The first publicly funded US police department was formed in Boston, Massachusetts, in 1838. It was the Boston police officers' job to protect the shipping industry and safeguard valuable goods coming in and out of the port.

THE DEFINITION OF POLICE BRUTALITY

Police brutality is excessive and unnecessary force against civilians. This can be physical or verbal assault. It can take place during an arrest or an interrogation. Sometimes people confuse excessive force with deadly force. The two are not the same. A police officer's behavior can be excessive without being deadly. When the tactics used exceed the type of force that is necessary to create a safe interaction, it is considered police brutality.

In the South, policing agencies served a different purpose and had a different target. Prior to the

Civil War (1861–1865) and the emancipation of enslaved people in 1865, it was a police officer's job to track down runaway slaves and crush slave revolts on white landowners' plantations. "Across the U.S., Black Americans lived in fear of law enforcement officials armed with weapons who monitored their every behavior, attacked them on the street and in their homes, and killed them for the slightest alleged provocation," writes *USA Today* reporter Wenei Philimon.[3]

THE GREAT MIGRATION

Decades after the Civil War, many formerly enslaved people relocated to Northern cities, seeking more opportunities and better lives than they had in the South. Called the Great Migration, it was the largest mass movement of people in US history. When it began in 1915, 90 percent of Black Americans lived in

Slave patrols were first formed in South Carolina in 1704. Although they were abolished once slavery became illegal in 1865, their tactics continued to influence those of hate groups such as the Ku Klux Klan.

the South. By the time the migration ended in the 1970s, 47 percent were living in the North and West.[5] In total, more than seven million Black people relocated. One prime destination was Chicago, Illinois. Between the years of 1915 and 1940, the Black population in that city more than doubled.[6]

Although Black people did find more jobs, housing, and cultural opportunities, they were still met with misfortune and prejudice, including from mostly white police departments. In 1929, for example, the Illinois Association for Criminal Justice published the Illinois Crime Survey. It analyzed the causes of high crime rates in Chicago and surrounding areas. The study also included data on police brutality. According to its findings, although Black people made up 5 percent of the region's population, they represented 30 percent of the victims of police killings.[7]

MEDIA SILENCE

Throughout US history, police brutality against Black people has been consistent. But in the 1900s, most white people didn't know how widespread the problem was. This is because many of the country's major newspapers, geared mostly toward white readers, didn't cover the events. In contrast, most Black-owned publications featured extensive coverage of police brutality against the Black community, often on the front page. It wasn't until televisions became popular and people increased their focus on civil rights issues during the 1960s that police brutality began to be covered on a more regular basis to a wider audience.

In the decades during and after World War II (1939–1945), tensions between police officers and Black communities escalated further. Black servicemen returned home from the war and expected to be treated as equal citizens under the Constitution. White-dominated police departments knew equality between people of color and white people would disrupt the racist social order they lived in. According to the Equal Justice Initiative, thousands of Black veterans throughout the South, parts of the Midwest, and the Northeast endured brutal attacks or died from mob-induced or police violence during this time.

RED SUMMER

World War II wasn't the first time Black servicemen were targeted after they returned home from fighting overseas. In the months following World War I (1914–1918), violence against Black veterans and their communities grew so bad that the period of time was called the Red Summer. Many whites were concerned that returning Black servicemen wouldn't resubmit to their former politically and socially inferior statuses.

One of the earliest incidents took place in Washington, DC, in July 1919. After a rumor circulated that a Black man had assaulted a white woman, intoxicated white sailors and army veterans went on a rampage throughout the city. They attacked and lynched Black people in the capital's streets. The mayhem spread to other US cities. Between April and November 1919, there were approximately 25 riots and instances of mob violence, and many recorded lynchings.[8]

The gradual change in demographics in cities inflamed police prejudices too, says Moore. In the 1940s and 1950s, neighborhoods in formerly white urban centers drew more Black residents. Many white people responded by moving away from this diversity into majority-white suburbs where they felt more comfortable. According to Moore, this shift made the Black population appear more threatening to white police officers. It also allowed law enforcement to feel more justified in using abusive tactics to control Black people's mobility and keep them in line. "The Great Migration [exposed] the racial divisions and disparities that in many ways continue to plague the nation and dominate headlines today, from police killings of unarmed African Americans to mass incarceration to widely documented biases in employment, housing, health care and education," writes *Smithsonian* magazine reporter Isabel Wilkerson.[9]

"TOO OFTEN PEOPLE LOOK AT THE CONTEMPORARY ISSUE, THE ISSUE THAT IS GOING ON RIGHT NOW BUT NOT UNDERSTANDING THAT ALL THAT IS HAPPENING IS STEEPED IN 400 YEARS OF LEGACY OF INJUSTICE. THESE PAST GRIEVANCES, PAST HARMS BY LAW ENFORCEMENT, NEED TO BE ADDRESSED BEFORE EVEN ATTEMPTING TO MOVE FORWARD."[10]

—JENNIFER COBBINA, A CRIMINAL JUSTICE PROFESSOR AT MICHIGAN STATE UNIVERSITY

CIVIL RIGHTS RACE RIOTS

By the 1960s, people of all races and backgrounds were fed up with inequalities in the United States. Communities of color rallied against segregation, discrimination, unfair housing policies, and unequal access to jobs and education. Though a lot of the civil rights movement's leaders advocated for peaceful demonstrations throughout this time period, many of the protests in cities across the United States turned violent.

In response, the police fought back with greater strength. They used fire hoses and tear gas to disperse protesters. Some unleashed police dogs into crowds at peaceful sit-ins, causing injuries to the participants.

This forceful response only inflamed people's frustrations, especially in communities of color. One of the deadliest riots took place in Detroit in 1967. On July 23, the police raided an illegal after-hours club in the mostly Black neighborhood of Virginia Park. People at the club had gathered to celebrate some war veterans. After the police arrived, several people were beaten or taken into custody. The next five days brought one of the most destructive riots in US history. More than 1,000 buildings were burned, 43 people—most of them Black—died, and more than 7,000 people were arrested.[11]

The Detroit riots were a result of years of built-up tension in the Black community over issues such as poverty, racism, and police brutality.

Nearly 25 years later, on March 3, 1991, a construction worker named Rodney King was beaten by members of the Los Angeles Police Department in California. He had raced away from police in his car at high speeds and was later charged with driving while intoxicated. When the police stopped King, they hit him with batons more than 50 times and stunned him with Tasers. The incident was caught on tape by a bystander and later aired on television. A year after the incident, three policemen involved in the beating were acquitted of all charges. The fourth officer had a mistrial. In protest, the people of Los Angeles rioted for five days. More than 50 people were killed and more than 2,300 were injured.[12]

PROPOSALS AFTER DETROIT

In response to the Detroit riots and others like them, President Lyndon B. Johnson created the National Advisory Commission on Civil Disorders in 1968. The commission concluded that out of 24 surveyed instances of riots and other types of civil unrest, half erupted in response to the police's abusive tactics. The committee made recommendations on how to reduce some of the tension between Black neighborhoods and majority-white police departments, including providing equal access to housing in low-income neighborhoods and bias training in police departments. President Johnson didn't act on the committee's suggestions.

Some people think police are going too far when they purchase military equipment. Others say that police need the equipment to be prepared for the worst.

DEATHS IN THE 2000s

For many decades, protests and riots in response to police violence have rocked the United States. But despite the reach of the protests and law enforcement's sometimes severe responses to them, police violence is still a significant issue.

Starting in 2015, the *Washington Post* began recording US police shootings that resulted in deaths. Between 2015 and 2020, it found that officers shot and killed approximately 1,000 people each year. According to the *Washington Post*, about 50 percent of those shot and killed were white people, who represent about 61 percent of the population. About 26 percent of those shot and killed were Black people, who represent less than 13 percent of the US population. Black people are more than twice as likely to be killed by police than white people are.[13] What these numbers make clear is that police brutality in the United States—especially against Black people—is still present.

What's more, some experts argue that the militarization of equipment the police use to quell riots and dole out punishments, such as high-tech body armor and armored vehicles, is likely exacerbating the issue rather than helping to solve it. "There's a reliance upon force that goes beyond what is necessary to accomplish police duty," says Malcolm D. Holmes, a sociology professor at the University of Wyoming.[14] Some people believe prime examples of this played out in cities throughout the United States after Floyd's death.

CHAPTER FOUR

PROTESTS AND
RIOTS IN
MINNEAPOLIS

I n the weeks leading up to George Floyd's death on May 25, 2020, the nation was like a tinderbox waiting to ignite. For one thing, stay-at-home orders in many states including Minnesota—enacted to combat the spread of COVID-19—had stretched on for weeks, and some for months. For another, on March 13 in Louisville, Kentucky, a 26-year-old Black emergency medical technician named Breonna Taylor was killed by police officers in her home. At around one in the morning, the police kicked in the door and entered. They had a no-knock warrant to search the premises for drugs and a known drug dealer named Jamarcus Glover, who was

A protester in Minneapolis walks past a burning building with an upside down US flag. Turning the flag like this is a symbol of distress.

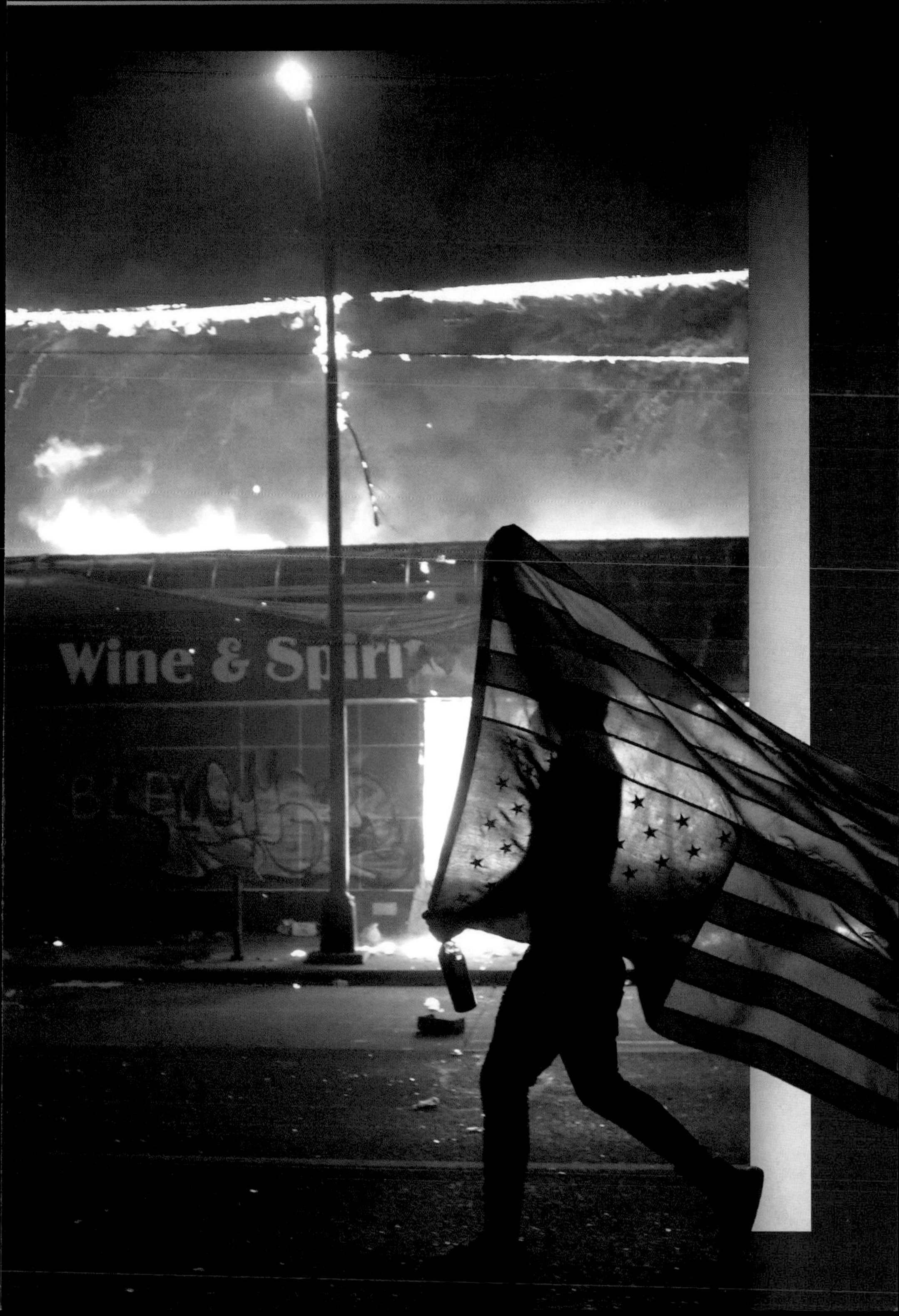
Wine & Spir

Taylor's ex-boyfriend. When Taylor's current boyfriend, Kenneth Walker, fired at the police because he thought the apartment was being burgled, the cops fired back and shot Taylor eight times.

Taylor's family filed a wrongful death lawsuit. Taylor didn't have any drugs in her apartment. She didn't live with Glover either. Civil rights attorney Ben Crump, the Taylors' lawyer, said the police supplied false information in order to get the search warrant approved. Taylor's family eventually won the lawsuit. They received $12 million from the city of Louisville.[1] The city also agreed to enact police reforms. In September 2020, a grand jury decided that the officers would not be charged with killing Taylor.

After Taylor's death, people in Louisville gathered in the streets to protest what had happened. But though the story made headlines in some news outlets, it hadn't gathered traction on a national scale. It wasn't until the video of Floyd's death surfaced on social media that people came out in full force to express their anger over the police's extreme behavior. The social unrest started in Minneapolis.

MORE TO THE
STORY

TOO MANY LIVES LOST

Prior to Floyd's death, people across the United States were fed up with how many Black people were getting killed by the police. One instance of police violence against a Black person occurred on August 9, 2014. Eighteen-year-old Michael Brown was apprehended in Ferguson, Missouri, for allegedly stealing a box of cigars. After a brief struggle, the police shot him six times. He died at the scene.

On November 22, 2014, 12-year-old Tamir Rice was shot in Cleveland, Ohio, after the police responded to a call that a male suspect who was "probably a juvenile" was pointing a gun that was "probably fake" at people passing by.[2] The police officers confirmed the gun was a toy only after they shot and killed Tamir.

On July 5, 2016, 37-year-old Alton Sterling was confronted by two white police officers while he was selling DVDs outside a convenience store in Baton Rouge, Louisiana. There was a scuffle, and one of the cops shot and killed Sterling. For various reasons, including claims of self-defense, none of the officers in these three cases were prosecuted.

In many police shootings, officers say they reacted out of fear for their lives. Police are allowed to use deadly force in self-defense or to protect other people. Some people say that bad policing is driving the number of police-involved shootings. "We have to get beyond what is legal and start focusing on what is preventable. Most [shootings] are preventable," said former East Palo Alto, California, police chief Ronald L. Davis.[3]

ANGER IN MINNEAPOLIS

By the afternoon of May 26, the day following Floyd's death, footage of the incident had already been viewed online thousands of times. Minneapolis police chief Medaria Arradondo fired the four officers involved. He also asked the Federal Bureau of Investigation (FBI) to look into what happened.

It soon became apparent that there were inconsistencies between what Monday's police report said and what appeared on video. For example, the report didn't mention any choke hold or knee-on-neck maneuver made by the cops. Instead, it stated that the suspect had a medical incident that resulted in his death. In a press conference announcing the police officers' termination that Tuesday, Minneapolis mayor Jacob Frey expressed his disapproval of the officers' behavior. "Every bit of what I saw was wrong. It was malicious. And it was unacceptable," he said. "There is no gray there."[4]

Meanwhile, hundreds of people started to gather in the area where Floyd was killed to pay their respects. Some left flowers and candles at the intersection where he died.

"BEING BLACK IN AMERICA SHOULD NOT BE A DEATH SENTENCE. . . . THIS IS NOT JUST THIS ONE INSTANCE THAT WE SHOULD BE ANGRY ABOUT. THESE ARE REPEATED INSTANCES WHERE BLACK MEN HAVE HAD THEIR LIVES TAKEN FROM THEM PREMATURELY, YES IN MINNESOTA AND ALL AROUND THE COUNTRY."[6]

—**MINNEAPOLIS MAYOR JACOB FREY**

Others marched in peaceful protests. People of all ages held handmade cardboard signs demanding justice. They shouted "I can't breathe" and "It could've been me" in unison.[5] Many people wore masks to protect themselves from COVID-19.

The next day, smaller groups of protesters organized in pockets throughout the city. Some stood outside Derek Chauvin's suburban home, splattered red paint on his driveway, and wrote "killer" on his garage door. Others went to Hennepin County attorney Mike Freeman's house

The intersection near Cup Foods was closed so people could protest Floyd's death. A memorial for Floyd was also created on the spot.

and demanded that the four officers be arrested. The protesters' loud, passionate voices and chanting could be heard for miles.

NIGHTTIME RIOTS

The marches on Tuesday and Wednesday morning were peaceful. But by Wednesday night, the situation had escalated. Some protesters spray-painted graffiti on squad cars parked on streets. Thousands of people crowded in front of the Third Precinct's police department, where the four officers had worked. Police dressed in riot gear and, holding massive shields, formed barricade lines in the street. At one point in the evening, the cops sprayed tear gas into the crowd in the hopes of dispersing it. They shot rubber bullets and threw flash grenades at protesters.

Some people began looting. They smashed store windows and stole merchandise from inside. They ransacked the Target store near the police building and branched out to other areas in the city. The looters stole televisions, clothing, diapers, and expensive sneakers. Others broke into a local liquor store and shattered windows at a market down the block. Many pharmacies were burglarized, with suspects seen running out of stores with armfuls of prescription pill bottles.

A PERMANENT MEMORIAL

After Floyd's death, thousands of people flocked to the intersection where the police altercation had occurred. They left flowers, candles, teddy bears, balloons, and hand-painted signs. On one nearby wall, local artists illustrated a replica of Floyd in vibrant colors with the phrase *I can breathe now* written underneath. In the image, Floyd's torso stands out against a circle with the names of many people who have died while in police custody.

The mural attracted so many visitors that there was talk of making the block a permanent memorial with a traffic roundabout, a peace garden, or a statue to honor Floyd's life. "I think ten years from now, 15 years from now, people will want to learn the history of what happened here and we want to be careful to preserve that in every way that we can," said Hennepin County commissioner Angela Conley.[7]

Minneapolis had also begun to burn. Rioters started a fire at an AutoZone store. Though firefighters tried to extinguish the blaze, the building was completely destroyed. A housing complex under construction was also targeted. The burning building's flames shot more than 100 feet (30 m) into the sky and engulfed an entire block.

Just before midnight, Mayor Jacob Frey made a plea to his city: "Please, please, Minneapolis. We cannot let tragedy beget more tragedy. . . . Please, help us keep the peace. Yes, we're reeling. I understand the anger and pain, and we need the public's help in keeping the peace tonight. We need that in order to get through this together."[8]

A CITY IN FLAMES

On Thursday, May 28, peaceful marches continued to throng the streets of Minneapolis during the day. Glass lay strewn across the pavement in areas throughout the city from the previous night's riots and looting. Many local businesses that hadn't yet been damaged boarded

Rioters stand outside a burning building in Minneapolis.

up their windows with plywood, and some spray-painted "Black-owned business" on the outside with the hopes of preventing further destruction.[10] Reports of the police clubbing rioters and making mass arrests made news headlines nationwide.

Then, on Thursday at around ten at night, rioters tore down a fence surrounding the Third Precinct building,

A CITY AT ODDS

Minneapolis is known for its culture and nightlife. But like many urban centers, it also has inequality. At the time of Floyd's death, the tension between people of different races—and between the public and the 800-member, mostly white police force—had been brewing in Minneapolis for quite some time.

Black people account for approximately 20 percent of the Minneapolis population. According to data released by the city's police department, they are more likely to be pulled over, arrested, and have force used against them than white residents. Between late 2009 and May 2019, Black people accounted for more than 60 percent of the victims in the city's police shootings. "The truth is we do not have a good history," said Jamar B. Nelson, a community activist who lives in the city. "The biggest complaint is that the community feels the police department is racist, bigoted, and uncaring about the Black community."[12]

causing the officers inside to leave. Then some of the crowd set fire to the building while others stood with their fists high and held signs that read "Enough is enough!"[11] Just a few hours later, much of the building had been destroyed.

By May 29, as many as 200 businesses in Minneapolis and St. Paul had been damaged. Tim Walz, the state's governor, activated the Minnesota National Guard and declared a state of emergency. Thousands of people continued to take to the streets and showed few signs of backing down. In fact, their calls for justice—some peaceful, some violent—had begun to spread throughout the country.

More than 1,000 National Guard members were deployed to Minneapolis.

FROM THE HEADLINES

SHOT WHILE JOGGING

Violence against Black people by those associated with law enforcement had led to passionate protests even earlier in 2020 and far south of Minneapolis. Ahmaud Arbery was 25 years old and lived with his mother outside Brunswick, Georgia. On February 23, 2020,

he decided to go for a jog in Satilla Shores, an affluent nearby neighborhood. Gregory McMichael spotted Arbery and believed he looked like a person suspected of home break-ins in the area.

McMichael was a former Glynn County police officer and investigator with the local district attorney's office. He called his son Travis and grabbed his handgun and a shotgun. The two hopped into a pickup truck and, joined by neighbor William Bryan in a different car, chased Arbery down. A video of the confrontation shows that after a brief scuffle, shots were fired, and Arbery fell to the ground. He later died from his wounds.

For two months, Arbery's death wasn't reported by the media. No arrests were made either. But after an article from the *New York Times* and the release of the video, the Georgia Bureau of Investigation was called in. On May 7, the police arrested the McMichaels and charged them with murder and aggravated assault. Protesters filled the streets to demand justice for Arbery.

Hundreds of people gathered to protest the death of Ahmaud Arbery on May 16, 2020.

CHAPTER FIVE

A NATION
DIVIDED

O n May 29, Americans woke up to the following news headline in the *New York Times*: "Ex-Officer Charged in Death of George Floyd in Minneapolis."[1] Derek Chauvin had been taken into custody and charged with third-degree murder and second-degree manslaughter. Months later, a judge dropped the third-degree charge but kept a higher-level second-degree charge.

Floyd's family members were outraged by what they considered too mild a charge. "We expected a first-degree murder charge. We want a first-degree murder charge," they wrote in an official statement.[2] The protesters in Minneapolis were upset too. Once again, they took to the streets and marched with signs,

Floyd's brother Philonise, *right*, and his sister, Bridgett, *left*, spoke at the March on Washington in August 2020.

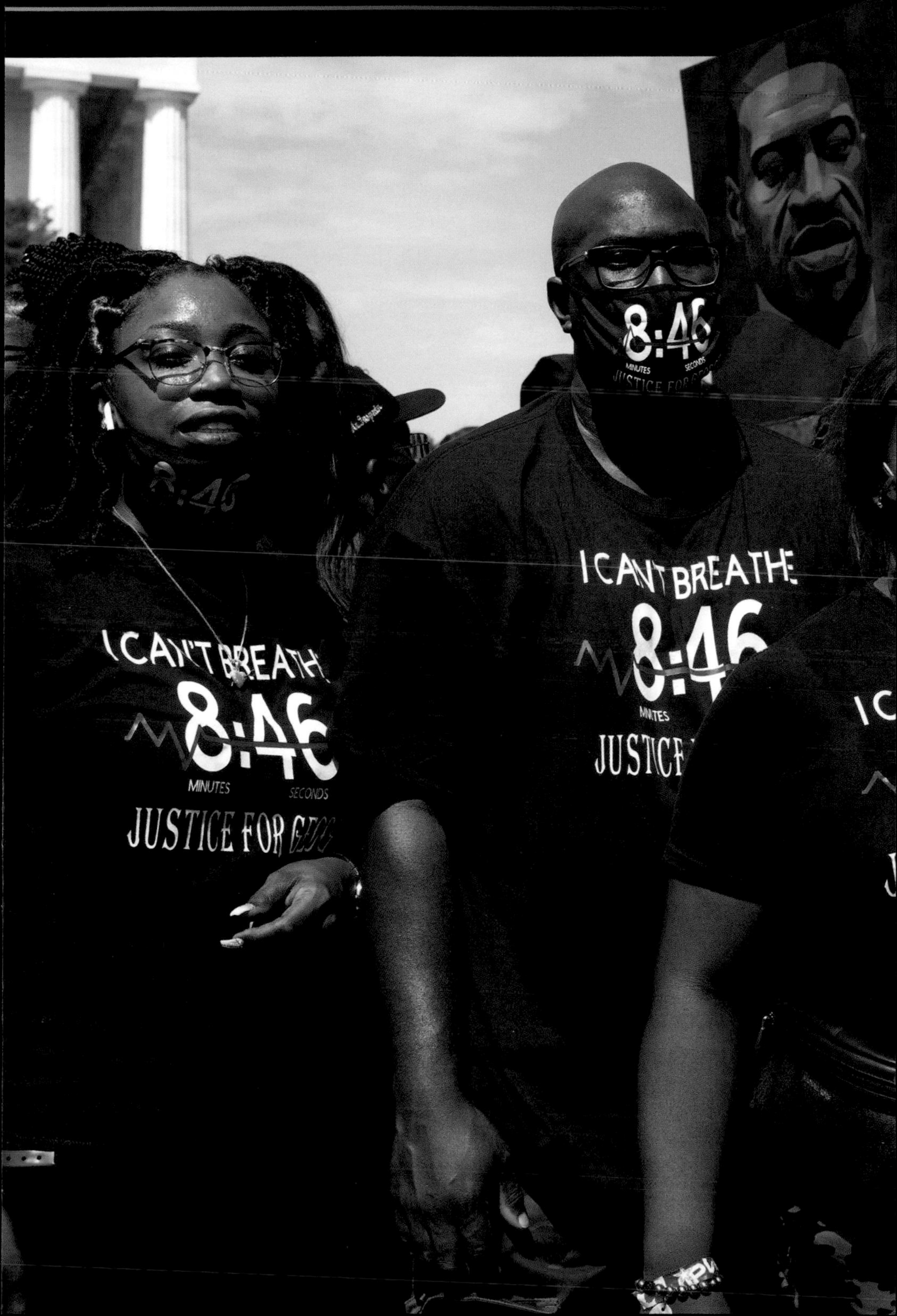
I CAN'T BREATHE
8:46
MINUTES
SECONDS
JUSTICE FOR

MURDER CHARGES EXPLAINED

On May 29, 2020, prosecutors charged former police officer Derek Chauvin with third-degree murder and second-degree manslaughter, which are less serious than a first- or second-degree murder charge. According to Richard Frase, a professor of criminal law at the University of Minnesota, a first-degree murder charge would require prosecutors to prove premeditation. In other words, they'd have to convince a jury that Chauvin intended to kill Floyd when he put his knee on Floyd's neck in order for Chauvin to be convicted.

Under Minnesota law, third-degree murder does not require an intent to kill. Instead, prosecutors must prove that the accused caused someone's death in a dangerous act "without regard for human life." For second-degree manslaughter, Chauvin's other charge, prosecutors needed to show that the officer was so reckless that he created an "unreasonable risk" and that he knew his actions might cause serious harm or death.[5]

yelling "I can't breathe" and "No justice, no peace."[3] Peaceful protests took place during the day, and violence and looting continued at night.

President Donald Trump threatened to use military force to quell the nightly riots. On Twitter, he called the protesters "thugs" and said, "When the looting starts, the shooting starts." Later, he sent another tweet: "I can't stand back & watch this happen to a great American City, Minneapolis. A total lack of leadership. Either the very weak Radical Left Mayor, Jacob Frey, get his act together and bring the City under control, or I will send in the National Guard & get the job done right."[4]

On May 30, Mayor Frey sent his own message to Minneapolis. He called the rioting a form of domestic terrorism and instituted an 8:00 p.m. curfew. Those who were caught breaking the curfew would be arrested.

UNIFIED IN PROTEST

Over the next week, daily marches sprang up in at least 140 big cities and small towns around the country. Many of the demonstrations during the day were peaceful. In Louisville, protesters mourned not only Floyd but also

Looters took advantage of the chaos in Minneapolis and began stealing from nearby stores, such as Target.

Breonna Taylor. In New York City, tens of thousands of people gathered and chanted "Get off our necks" and "Racism is America's original sin."[6] They held up signs that read "Stop killing us" and staged protests that stretched across the city's iconic bridges.[7]

In Denver, Colorado, players and coaches from the Broncos football team participated in a march from the state capitol to Civic Center Park downtown. In Portland, Oregon, daily demonstrations lasted for months, and federal officers were called in to protect federal buildings. There, and in other cities, government officials ordered police officers to stop using chemical weapons such as tear gas and pepper spray against peaceful protesters. "Our community has serious concerns about the use of [tear gas] for crowd management, particularly during a time when we're battling a pandemic," said Portland mayor Ted Wheeler. "Gas should not be used unless there is a serious and immediate threat

"I'M FEELING [THE PROTESTERS'] GROWING TENSION. IT IS DIFFICULT TO BE A BLACK AMERICAN AT THE MOMENT. WE ARE GETTING HIT HARD. WE ARE SEEING THAT OUR LIVES ARE NOT VALUED."[8]

—CITY COUNCILPERSON DONOVAN RICHARDS, IN QUEENS, NEW YORK CITY

to life safety, and there is no other viable alternative for dispersal."[9]

Other events happened in Washington, DC. In one instance, more than 10,000 people gathered outside the White House to protest President Trump's inaction and demand justice, causing the Secret Service to temporarily lock down the building. Demonstrators later marched down U Street's historic Black Broadway and met at the Lincoln Memorial. Local artists and city workers painted "Black Lives Matter" in bright yellow letters on the pavement in front of Lafayette Square. Nearby, activists painted a different, unauthorized slogan: "Defund the police."[10]

TRUMP AND PROTESTERS

On Monday, June 1, 2020, a large crowd gathered in Lafayette Park in front of the White House for the third day in a row. They shouted for justice, chanting, "Say his name: George Floyd!"[11] That day, US attorney general William Barr ordered the police to clear the park. Around six thirty that evening, the officers fired flash grenades, rubber bullets, and tear gas into the crowd. Many demonstrators were injured. Once the park was cleared, Trump walked to the nearby historic St. John's Church and posed for a photo holding a Bible.

After the event, the American Civil Liberties Union and other activist organizations criticized Trump for what they saw as a harsh approach toward protesters. For his part, earlier that day Trump had criticized local and state leaders for not doing enough to calm the riots in their cities and states. He advocated for officials to use greater force.[12]

THE VIOLENCE CONTINUES

Amid the protests, a number of other big developments occurred. On June 1, Terrence Floyd visited the site where his brother died—the first in his family to do so. With tears in his eyes, he begged demonstrators to honor his brother using peaceful means, not violence. That same day, two official autopsies were released. Both said Floyd's death was a homicide.

"IF I'M NOT OVER HERE BLOWING UP STUFF, IF I'M NOT OVER HERE MESSING UP MY COMMUNITY, THEN WHAT ARE YOU ALL DOING? WHAT ARE YOU ALL DOING? YOU ALL DOING NOTHING! BECAUSE THAT'S NOT GOING TO BRING MY BROTHER BACK AT ALL."[13]

—TERRENCE FLOYD, GEORGE FLOYD'S BROTHER, TO RIOTERS

On June 3, Tou Thao, J. Alexander Kueng, and Thomas Lane were charged with aiding and abetting second-degree murder and manslaughter. Chauvin's charges were also increased to second-degree murder. This pushed his possible prison sentence to 40 years.

Despite these developments, the tension between police and demonstrators increased. Mayors in cities across the United States issued mandatory evening curfews in hopes of preventing more looting and vandalism.

But many rioters continued to inflict damages after dark. While some police officers didn't engage in violence and even seemed to align with some of the peaceful protesters, others beat up demonstrators and sprayed people, including journalists, with pepper spray.

In Buffalo, New York, for example, officers Aaron Torgalski and Robert McCabe were suspended without pay and charged with felony assault after shoving 75-year-old Martin Gugino to the ground. In Fort Lauderdale, Florida,

Even though cities began imposing curfews, many people who intended to protest peacefully, including those in Minneapolis, stayed on the streets.

MORE TO THE
STORY

A HEATED DEBATE

As marches and demonstrations grew violent and looting occurred in the days and nights after Floyd's death, many people argued about what kinds of protests were morally acceptable. Some people saw vandalism and looting as forms of empowerment. "When you have the ability to gain some of that power back, people take the opportunity to do so," said Rashawn Ray, a sociologist at the University of Maryland.[14] Some people also insisted extreme circumstances called for extreme measures. Looting, they believed, was the only way to make their voices heard. "In Baltimore, they've been saying for generations how bad the Baltimore Police Department was, but nobody listened," said Lorenzo Boyd, the director of the Center for Advanced Policing at the University of New Haven. "And then Freddie Gray got killed, and nobody listened. And then they started protesting; nobody listened. But as soon as the CVS burned in Baltimore, the whole world watched."[15]

However, other people felt peaceful protests were the only way to get things done. Vandalism and looting can have harmful consequences for residents. For instance, Stephanie Wilford lived in Minneapolis where the rioting occurred. When interviewed, she wept openly on television, saying that she was terrified during the riots. She also noted that all the stores she shopped at were destroyed and public transportation was shut down: "[The rioters] are tearing up our livelihood . . . and now I don't have anywhere to go."[16]

officers shot a nonviolent protester in the head with foam rubber bullets, fracturing her eye socket. "It feels like the police are being challenged in ways that they haven't been challenged in some time," said Chuck Wexler, the executive director of the Police Executive Research Forum. "They are responding. And sometimes, that response is totally inappropriate."[17]

Judging from the turbulent events that transpired at the end of May and the beginning of June, it was clear that Floyd's death had opened the floodgates of discontent in the United States. These sentiments were reflected in countries around the world.

Some people poured milk on their faces after getting hit with pepper spray to try and take away some of the sting.

FROM THE
HEADLINES

GEORGE FLOYD
LAID TO REST

Many memorials were held for Floyd. One was in
Minneapolis, and another took place in Raeford,
North Carolina, near where Floyd was born. On
June 9, 2020, Floyd was laid to rest in his
hometown of Houston. His body was transported
to the cemetery in a gold casket inside a
gleaming-white, horse-drawn carriage. He was
buried in the Houston Memorial Gardens next to
his mother's grave. Thousands of people watched
the procession.

The service at Fountain of Praise Church
featured multiple speakers and civil rights leaders,
such as former vice president Joe Biden, Texas
representatives Al Green and Sheila Jackson Lee,
and Houston mayor Sylvester Turner. Relatives
who had lost loved ones because of police

Minneapolis mayor Jacob Frey, *kneeling*,
pays his respects at Floyd's Minneapolis
memorial service on June 4, 2020.

brutality also attended, as well as celebrities such as actor Jamie Foxx and singer Ne-Yo.

Floyd's family members told stories of the "gentle giant" and demanded justice for his premature death. Civil rights activist Rev. Al Sharpton also gave a heartfelt and fiery speech, echoing the thoughts of many in the room and around the world: "God took the rejected stone and made him the cornerstone of a movement that's going to change the whole wide world," he said. "Your family is going to miss you George, but your nation is going to always remember your name. Because your neck was one that represents all of us, and how you suffered is how we all suffer."[18]

CHAPTER SIX

GLOBAL
SUPPORT

O n Wednesday, June 17, more than three weeks after his older brother's death, Philonise Floyd had a message for the international community. By video, he gave a passionate speech to the United Nations Human Rights Council in Geneva, Switzerland. In it, he asked the group for help. "My brother, George Floyd, is one of the many Black men and women that have been murdered by police in recent years. The sad truth is that the case is not unique," he said. "The way you saw my brother tortured and murdered on camera is the way Black people are treated by police in America."[1]

Philonise then asked the council to set up an independent task force that would look into systemic

Philonise's plea to the United Nations was answered when the council decided to investigate and then report on racism in various countries.

CHEF DE BRANCHE

racism in the United States and provide recommendations for how to address the problem. He pleaded with them to investigate law enforcement's persistent killing of Black people. He called for an end to the violence being used against peaceful demonstrators in the protests sweeping the nation. Most of all, he wanted the victims of police brutality to see justice and their families to be given reparations for their suffering.

"YOU IN THE UNITED NATIONS, YOU ARE YOUR BROTHERS' AND SISTERS' KEEPERS IN AMERICA AND YOU HAVE THE POWER TO HELP US GET JUSTICE FOR MY BROTHER GEORGE FLOYD. I AM ASKING YOU TO HELP HIM. I AM ASKING YOU TO HELP ME. I AM ASKING YOU TO HELP US: BLACK PEOPLE IN AMERICA."[2]

—PHILONISE FLOYD IN A SPEECH TO THE UNITED NATIONS HUMAN RIGHTS COUNCIL

The leader of the group, former Chilean president Michelle Bachelet, sympathized with Philonise's requests and pledged the council's support. "We should go beyond existing recommendations. We need to build on what has worked from the enormous body of work and experience we already have," she said to the assembled diplomats at the meeting. "Time is of the essence. Patience has run out. Black lives matter. Indigenous lives matter . . . people of color matter. All human beings are born equal in dignity and rights."[3]

A WORLDWIDE RECKONING

News of Floyd's death—and Americans' reaction to it—reached the farthest corners of the world. By mid-June, people in countries far and wide had joined the fight for a more equitable world and begun protesting the death of not just Floyd but also others like him in their own countries.

In Paris, France, nearly 20,000 people showed up in front of the Tribunal de Paris on June 2.[4] They congregated to support protest organizer Assa Traoré, whose brother Adama died on July 19, 2016, after being restrained by police. "We *are* Black Lives Matter," Traoré told the *New Yorker* magazine. "The two

PHILONISE APPEALS TO THE US HOUSE OF REPRESENTATIVES

On June 10, the US House of Representatives Judiciary Committee held a hearing on police brutality in the United States. Lawmakers spoke about issues such as police department budgets, the prevalence of racial profiling, and how ingrained racial biases in police departments affect communities of color. Those impacted by police violence also spoke, including Philonise Floyd. He testified that former officer Chauvin had lynched his brother.

"I'm tired of pain, pain you feel when you watch something like that, when you watch your big brother, who you've looked up to your whole life, die. George wasn't hurting anyone that day. . . . I'm asking you: Is that what a black man is worth—$20? This is 2020," Philonise said. "By speaking to you today, maybe I can make sure his life was not in vain."[5]

Countries in Europe, such as France, also struggle with racism against people of color.

fights echo each other, so that we're pulling back the curtain on France, in saying, 'People of the whole world, look what's happening here.'"[6]

In Mexico City, Mexico, thousands of people marched for construction worker Giovanni Lopez, who was allegedly beaten to death while in police custody. They vandalized the US embassy, and the building was put on lockdown. Crowds also gathered in Toronto, Canada,

MORE TO THE
STORY

TAKING A KNEE
IN PROTEST

When the Floyd protests started, images surfaced of demonstrators and cops alike down on one knee. So, what does it mean to take a knee in protest? The move's origin can be attributed to football quarterback Colin Kaepernick. On August 26, 2016, he sat on the bench during the playing of the US national anthem prior to a game. On September 1, he switched to getting down on one knee. "I am not going to stand up to show pride in a flag for a country that oppresses Black people and people of color," he said at the time.[7]

Some fans criticized Kaepernick for being unpatriotic. National Football League (NFL) commissioner Roger Goodell said, "I don't necessarily agree with what [Kaepernick] is doing. . . . I support our players when they want to see change in society, and we don't live in a perfect society. On the other hand, we believe very strongly in patriotism in the NFL. I personally believe very strongly in that."[8] But in the years since then, taking a knee has become a powerful show of solidarity for the Black Lives Matter movement.

Though many fans remained critical of protests during NFL games, Goodell expressed an updated opinion following George Floyd's death, saying he had come to believe that Kaepernick and other players who joined him in kneeling were "not people who are unpatriotic. They're not disloyal. They're not against our military. . . . What they're trying to do is exercise their right to bring attention to something that needs to get fixed."[9]

in memory of Regis Korchinski-Paquet, who fell from an apartment building after the police arrived to look into what they say was a domestic assault concern.

There were demonstrations in Germany, Spain, the Netherlands, England, and Scotland. People also took to the streets in Osaka, Japan; Pristina, Kosovo; and in countries such as Zimbabwe and Kenya. In South Africa, demonstrators shouted for justice for Collins Khosa. He died after soldiers in the South Africa National Defense Force found a half-finished glass of alcohol in his yard and accused him of violating the coronavirus quarantine. They reportedly choked him, slammed him against a cement wall, knocked him over the head with

INDECISION IN AUSTRALIA

By the first week in June 2020, protests over Floyd's death were raging all over the world—but so was the coronavirus. As early as March, leaders of many countries had ordered their citizens not to leave their homes in order to protect themselves from infection. Now those same leaders were worried the protests and riots would cause a spike in COVID-19 cases.

On Friday, June 6, an Australian court ruled that marches could not be held in the country because of the need for social distancing. The next day, a higher court rejected the ruling, saying protests could indeed go on. But people had vowed to protest no matter what the courts ruled. Crowds of tens of thousands of mask-wearing people gathered in Sydney, Melbourne, and elsewhere throughout the country to demand change.

a machine gun, and poured liquor over him as police officers watched.

CALLING OUT PAST RACISM

People in Europe, South America, Asia, and elsewhere weren't just protesting police killings. The timing of Floyd's death had thrown harsh spotlights on the entrenched prejudices and racist practices that had existed in some countries for centuries. "With the coronavirus pandemic laying bare systemic inequalities and racial discrimination, people around the world are seizing the moment to push for change in their own countries," wrote *Time* reporter Suyin Haynes. "As they stand in solidarity with protesters in the U.S., they're also calling for a reckoning with past and contemporary injustices."[10]

"WE STAND WITH OUR KITH AND KIN IN AMERICA IN THESE DIFFICULT AND TRYING TIMES, AND WE HOPE THAT THE UNFORTUNATE, TRAGIC DEATH OF GEORGE FLOYD WILL INSPIRE A LASTING CHANGE IN HOW AMERICA CONFRONTS HEAD ON THE PROBLEMS OF HATE AND RACISM."[11]

—GHANA PRESIDENT NANA AKUFO-ADDO

On June 7, a 125-year-old statue of Edward Colston, who made his fortune in the 1600s as a slave trader in West Africa, was torn down in the English port city of Bristol. In Brussels, Belgium, people

railed against the reign of King Leopold II, who ruled

over the Congo for more than 20 years beginning in 1885, during which time an estimated ten million Congolese were killed. And in Antwerp, Belgium, a statue of the king was permanently taken down after being lit on fire the week prior. "The protesters were doing an incredible job in calling out King Leopold for what he is: a colonizer and a genocider," said Brussels-based scholar Adeola Aderemi.[12]

COVID-19 AND RACIAL DISPARITIES

Studies have shown that some racial and ethnic groups are affected more than others by the COVID-19 pandemic. According to the *New York Times*, Black and Hispanic people in the United States are three times as likely to become infected as their white neighbors and nearly twice as likely to die from the virus as white people.[13] This is because of a number of factors. One is unequal access to health care. Black and Hispanic people are also more likely to have customer service jobs, which makes them more exposed to the virus than their white counterparts who can work from home. Many live in cramped apartments or multigenerational homes. Many also rely on public transportation to get around. These factors also increase their potential for exposure.

As in the United States, people across the globe were demanding an end to police violence and the complete overhaul of a world in which they perceive Black people and people of color are treated as inferior and not given the freedoms they

A statue of King Leopold II was vandalized with red paint to signify the blood on his hands during his rule over the Congo.

deserve. "What comes next is uncertain—whether protests will continue, whether there will be real change," wrote Jen Kirby, a reporter for Vox. "At this moment, though, 'Black Lives Matter' is a global rallying cry and a gut-punch reminder that this message still needs to be repeated everywhere."[14]

RHODES MUST FALL

In early June 2020, more than 1,000 protesters at Oxford University in England staged a peaceful sit-in. They shouted "Take it down" and demanded the removal of a campus statue of the 1800s British imperialist Cecil Rhodes. Though the Rhodes Must Fall campaign had been trying to get the word out about their cause since the movement started in Cape Town, South Africa, in 2015, it took the Floyd uprising for the rest of the world to notice. "Rhodes represents such a violent legacy of colonialism, imperialism, slavery, particularly in southern Africa. . . . Take down a statue that celebrates that," said Morategi Kale, who participated in the protest and is a South African student at Oxford.[15]

FROM THE HEADLINES

BLACK LIVES MATTER: A BRIEF HISTORY

Black Lives Matter (BLM) is a movement that was founded in 2013 by Alicia Garza, Opal Tometi, and Patrisse Cullors after the killing of Trayvon Martin, an unarmed, Black 17-year-old from Miami Gardens, Florida. Martin was fatally shot in Sanford, Florida, by George Zimmerman, a neighborhood watchman. Zimmerman was acquitted of all charges.

BLM, with a presence in the United States, United Kingdom, and Canada, says its mission is to "eradicate white supremacy and build local power to intervene in violence inflicted on Black communities by the state and vigilantes."[16] It began as a small, chapter-based organization that aimed to expand and connect people in countries all over the world.

Since its formation, BLM has motivated hundreds of thousands of people around the world to fight for its cause. Among other protests, it staged the 2014 Black Lives Matter Freedom Ride, in which hundreds of people traveled from

The BLM movement has helped mobilize people to fight racial injustices.

Los Angeles, Chicago, Houston, and other cities to Ferguson, Missouri, to protest the shooting death of unarmed Black teen Michael Brown by white Ferguson police officer Darren Wilson. In June 2018, people participating in a BLM protest swarmed the San Diego, California, border with Mexico and demanded the humane treatment of migrants and refugees seeking asylum in the United States. And three months later, BLM members constructed 175 makeshift caskets and placed them outside a police conference held in Sacramento, California. According to a BLM spokesperson, the coffins represented the Black people killed by police in the city. The move was also a tribute to Stephon Clark, who was fatally shot by the Sacramento police outside his grandparents' home during a vandalism investigation in 2018.

CHAPTER SEVEN

A CALL FOR
REFORM

A ccording to national data, fatal shootings by the police have taken place in every state in the United States. They happen more frequently in cities with high population density. Local and federal investigations also show that systemic racial biases exist in many law enforcement offices, including those in Chicago; Baltimore, Maryland, where Freddie Gray died in police custody in 2015; and Ferguson, Missouri. Among 2018 residents of Ferguson, where Michael Brown was killed, a Black motorist was more than three times as likely as a white driver to be pulled over.

In New York City, police stopped Black and Hispanic drivers at much higher rates too. "About 83 percent of the stops during about a decade-long period

According to a 2020 analysis by ABC News, Black people in the United States are five times more likely to get arrested than white people are.

WHO WAS FREDDIE GRAY?

On April 12, 2015, 25-year-old Freddie Gray was arrested by the Baltimore Police Department for possessing a knife. The cops put him in the police van. Forty-five minutes later, he was found unconscious and not breathing. His spinal cord had been nearly severed. After a seven-day coma, Gray died on April 19.

A bystander video of Gray's encounter with the police was uploaded onto social media and quickly went viral. It showed him being held facedown on the sidewalk by officers Garrett Miller and Edward Nero. Gray's ankles were crossed and his knees bent. Miller's heels were shoved into Gray's back.

On May 1, the state prosecutor announced criminal charges against the six police officers involved. After multiple court cases and investigations, the officers were acquitted of some of the charges in Gray's death. The other charges were dropped.

involved Black[s] and Hispanics, even though they make up about 50 percent of the city's residents," reported Michael Barbaro of the *New York Times*. "And in Minneapolis, [as of June 2020] data showed that use of force against Black people in that city was seven times greater than it was against white people in the city. . . . All of that data seems to point to a pattern of racial discrimination."[1]

In the days and months following George Floyd's death, there was much deliberation about whether a pattern of racial discrimination in police stops, use of force, and arrests actually exists in the United States or whether the police are just doing their jobs. Many people wondered whether police departments should be reformed, and if so, what those reforms should entail.

Some put out calls to defund the police entirely, while others questioned whether that was a realistic solution given the crime in certain neighborhoods and the need for community protection.

The discussion is complicated. For one, almost all policing is done at the local and state levels, not federal. What that means is different laws exist for different states. Reaching a consensus on what steps to take as a nation can be difficult. What's allowed in one municipality might not be legal in another.

Police officers are charged with protecting and serving their communities.

Secondly, some people say aggressive, racist behavior against people of color by law enforcement is not a systemic problem, but just a case of, as national security adviser Robert O'Brien says, "a few bad apples."[2] In other words, these people believe that most cops are there to uphold the safety of their communities. The officers who act out or display prejudicial tendencies are just outliers on the force.

Thirdly, there are people who don't dispute the data but also don't believe the shootings are an issue of race. "I personally don't ever see race. I never have. I've been in law enforcement for over 30 years. I don't care what's your color, creed, race. It doesn't matter. You're a human being . . . and I will act the same way you act towards me," said Vince Champion, southeast regional director for the International Brotherhood of Police Officers. "If we're cordial, we're talking, we're going to be cordial and talking. If you're

"NOBODY REALLY WANTS TO TALK ABOUT HOW MANY TIMES OFFICERS HAVE STEPPED IN AND PROTECTED PEOPLE FROM RACISM. AND NOBODY KNOWS ABOUT IT, BECAUSE, YOU KNOW WHY? BECAUSE THAT'S OUR JOB."[3]

—VINCE CHAMPION, SOUTHEAST REGIONAL DIRECTOR FOR THE INTERNATIONAL BROTHERHOOD OF POLICE OFFICERS

going to fight me, I'm going to defend myself."[4] Regardless of a person's view on the issue, it is clear that police reform is complex. According to experts, three of the main debates are centered around the power of police unions, the existence of qualified immunity, and the proposal to defund law enforcement.

THE POWER OF POLICE UNIONS

In the United States, police unions protect law enforcement officers. It's the union's job to safeguard the officers' rights and ensure they receive due process under the law no matter what. "A major role for police unions is basically as an insurance policy," said Dale Belman, a labor relations professor at Michigan State University. "The feeling of a lot of officers is that it's very easy to sacrifice them. Something goes wrong and boom."[5]

But many people who are critical of police unions say this protection sometimes goes too far. For example, police unions have the power to prevent the public from seeing how many complaints have been filed against officers. They can erase an officer's disciplinary record after a few years or delay the questioning of an officer for up

MORE TO THE
STORY

PROTECTING
THE UNIFORM

In 2017, Reuters conducted a study on police union contracts in 82 cities across the United States. In a majority of those cities, the police departments were legally allowed to erase the disciplinary records of police officers. In 20 cities, such as San Antonio, Texas, cops accused of bad behavior were allowed to give up sick leave or vacation time instead of serving a suspension. Eighteen cities required an accused officer's written consent before the police department would release any disciplinary or internal investigation records to the public. Almost half of the contracts studied allowed officers to view everything in their file, including witness statements, photos, or videos, before being interviewed about a case or complaint. "The balance has dramatically shifted . . . to the creation of barriers to actual accountability that don't serve the public good," said Jonathan Smith, former chief of special litigation in the Civil Rights Division of the US Department of Justice.[6]

However, some people note that police union contracts give necessary protections to officers. Rick Weisman is the director of labor services at the National Fraternal Order of Police. He said, "Our job isn't to keep bad officers in this profession. Our job is to make sure that due process is given to the officers."[7]

to 48 hours after an incident. "They have these unusual protections they've bargained very hard for, measures that insulate them from accountability," said William P. Jones, a history professor at the University of Minnesota.[8]

Union leaders have also been known to use the money from high membership dues—a yearly amount members pay to belong to the union—to block police reform legislation or put pressure on politicians who are not acting in the best interest of their local police department. For example, Minneapolis city councilmember Steve Fletcher tried to direct money away from hiring police officers and toward a newly created office of violence prevention. In retaliation, Fletcher alleged, the police stopped responding as quickly to 911 calls placed by the people in Fletcher's community.

THE DEBATE OVER QUALIFIED IMMUNITY

One of the biggest debates surrounding police reform involves qualified immunity. Under most union contracts, qualified immunity protects officers from legal ramifications unless a person can prove that his or her constitutional rights were violated. According to the

New York Times, most cops who commit violent acts aren't criminally prosecuted for their actions. For example, out of 1,147 people killed in the United States by the police in 2017, officers were charged with a crime in 13 of the cases, or about 1 percent of the time.[9] This low rate of prosecution prevents family members of the victims from receiving compensation for their loved ones' deaths. Even in the rare cases where the cops involved in the incident are charged, such as in George Floyd's death, those officers can use the qualified immunity defense in most states.

Steve Fletcher became a member of the Minneapolis City Council in 2018.

There are two major sides of the qualified immunity discussion. Proponents say the practice is necessary because police officers face life-or-death situations every day. Without qualified immunity, they would be less able to make split-second decisions because of the fear of being reprimanded. As a result, fewer people might be interested in joining the police force. Opponents of qualified immunity argue it prevents officers from being held accountable. They say it gives officers a free pass to do anything they want because they might get away with it.

The debate is unresolved. On June 19, 2020, Colorado became the first US state to strip police officers of qualified immunity. In late June 2020, House Democrats submitted a bill that aimed to address the issue of qualified immunity and compensation for cases of wrongful death and police misconduct. Senate Republicans also submitted a competing bill that would, in part, help fund more training efforts to teach officers how to handle difficult situations without using force. Democratic senators voted to block the Republican bill from moving forward. In October 2020, the Democratic bill was still alive, but the

Republican-controlled Senate said it would not pass the bill. In late 2020, it appeared that any police reform bills were at a standstill.

COMPETING REFORM BILLS

In late June 2020, members of Congress submitted two bills geared toward police reform. Both proposals stipulated that police agencies collect and report more data about police activity, especially the use of excessive force. They would institute increased training and incentives for cops to wear body cameras. They also would make lynching a federal crime.

But the Democratic and Republican bills also differed in a number of key suggestions. Democrats demanded an end to choke holds; Republicans aimed to narrow restrictions on when choke holds could be used. Democrats wanted victims of police brutality or their relatives to be able to sue officers accused of police brutality, while Republicans insisted that qualified immunity should still be permissible. Democrats wanted to make the process of prosecuting police misconduct easier. Republicans preferred to focus on de-escalation training to prevent bad behavior from happening.

DEFUNDING THE POLICE

Every year in the United States, the total amount of funding distributed to police departments nationwide is about $100 billion. The Minneapolis Police Department, which employed 892 sworn officers and 175 civilian employees, received about $193.3 million in 2020.[10] Police funding is used for things such as training, uniforms and weapons, health benefits, salaries, and pensions.

But after Floyd's death, groups across the country started asking for the distribution of funds to be reexamined. As in every aspect of police reform, there are many opinions about the issue. Some argue the current way the police departments are run—and the amount of money they receive every year from the government—is fine. "Defunding will have an adverse effect on citizens most in need of police protection," said Law Enforcement Legal Defense Fund president Jason C. Johnson and retired FBI supervisory special agent James A. Gagliano. "Federal lawmakers must find the courage to implement and fund a series of long-overdue reforms that effectively reset, and make uniform, professional standards. This is the only feasible and realistic path forward."[11]

"[DEFUNDING LAW ENFORCEMENT] MEANS THAT WE ARE REDUCING THE ABILITY FOR LAW ENFORCEMENT TO HAVE RESOURCES THAT HARM OUR COMMUNITIES. IT'S ABOUT REINVESTING THOSE DOLLARS INTO BLACK COMMUNITIES, COMMUNITIES THAT HAVE BEEN DEEPLY DIVESTED FROM."[12]

—PATRISSE CULLORS, COFOUNDER OF THE BLACK LIVES MATTER MOVEMENT

Advocates who support the defunding of police departments say too much money is going toward policing in general, especially given recent examples of police misconduct. They support reform that would take some of the money from city budgets that would normally go to police departments and allocate it for other community uses, such as programs that combat homelessness and domestic violence, mental health initiatives, or funding for local schools. Other ideas include investing in social services in some of the poorer, marginalized communities where much of the strictest policing happens. "We're asking cops to do too much in this country," Dallas police chief David Brown said in 2016. "Every societal failure, we put it off on the cops to solve. . . . That's too much to ask. Policing was never meant to solve all those problems."[13]

The most radical activists want governments to disband police departments altogether. Instead, first

THE CITY THAT DISBANDED THE POLICE FORCE

In 2010, Camden, New Jersey, was considered one of the most dangerous and drug-ridden cities in the country. Almost 40 percent of residents lived below the poverty line. The police department was known for fabricating evidence and using excessive force.

In 2013, the city police department was eliminated and instead put under county control. All the cops were laid off and had to reapply for jobs. Their salaries were lower, and they weren't protected by a union. New bias training initiatives and community-focused programs were put into place. Complaints of excessive use of force dropped dramatically. During the first years of the county force, there were 35 to 65 a year. In the first half of 2020, there were fewer than five.[14]

responders to nonviolent 911 calls would be mental health providers, social workers, or other types of victim advocates. For example, trained medical professionals would respond to drug overdose situations instead of police officers.

It remains to be seen what the full response will be from state governments and which measures they will take to reform their police departments. There is still a strong push for reform. The conversations and negotiations taking place are a start.

Some people want the New York Police Department, the country's biggest police force, to receive less funding. They want the money to go to educational and social programs instead.

CHAPTER EIGHT

GEORGE FLOYD'S
LEGACY

T he killing of a Black man by law enforcement is not a new occurrence in the United States. But never in the past few decades has a death sparked such a widespread and long-lasting response as Floyd's has. In total, there were protests in all 50 states, in more than 2,000 cities nationwide, and in more than 60 countries. In August 2020, tens of thousands of protesters in Portland, Seattle, Chicago, and other major cities were still taking to the streets to demand not just incremental adjustments to the way police departments were run but the full-blown dismantling of what they saw as dysfunctional systems.

Floyd's death sparked civil rights movements across the globe, and many people hoped his death would bring about real change for people of color.

"In a span of mere days, the death of a Black man with a white policeman's knee on his neck became a parable in America's aching racial story and a rallying point for action that resonated far beyond Minnesota, where he died, and disrupted politics, business, culture and sports," wrote CNN correspondent Stephen Collinson.[1]

In the months after Floyd's death, various police reform proposals were introduced. Some cities banned choke holds. School districts in many towns and urban areas stopped having officers stationed in school buildings. President Trump signed an executive order that set up a national database to track police misconduct. But beyond these initiatives, Floyd's legacy affected many other aspects of US life, including street names and flags, corporate messaging, and entertainment and sports.

NEW STREET NAMES AND FLAGS

In June 2020, Washington, DC, mayor Muriel Bowser became the first city leader to rename a portion of a city to reflect the growing movement. A two-block section of Sixteenth Street NW in downtown Washington, on the north side of Lafayette Park, was officially christened Black Lives Matter Plaza. In New York City, Mayor Bill de Blasio came up with the idea to name one street in each of the city's five boroughs Black Lives Matter Street. Activists in the city also painted Black Lives Matter in giant yellow letters on the pavement in front of Trump Tower.

Another major symbolic change happened when Mississippi's state government decided to revamp the design of its state flag. It was the last flag in the United States to feature the Confederate battle emblem, a symbol of the group of Southern states that fought partly to uphold slavery during the Civil

SAFE POLICING FOR SAFE COMMUNITIES

On June 16, 2020, President Trump signed into law an executive order called Safe Policing for Safe Communities. It would create a database designed to keep track of any misconduct a police officer engaged in while on the job. It called on police departments to ban the use of choke holds except in life-endangering situations. It also pushed departments to send certain 911 calls to social workers and mental health professionals in cases of addiction or homelessness.

Many people praised the order. Republican representative Jim Jordan called it a "tremendous step forward in improving the system and beginning a new era in the relationship between communities and the police officers that keep them safe." But there were critics too. House Speaker Nancy Pelosi, a Democrat, said, "The President's weak Executive Order falls sadly and seriously short of what is required to combat the epidemic of racial injustice and police brutality that is murdering hundreds of Black Americans."[3]

War. On June 30, the bill was signed into law and a new design was already underway. "I also understand the need to commit the 1894 flag to history and find a banner that is a better emblem for all Mississippi," said Mississippi governor Tate Reeves.[4]

THE DEBATE OVER THE CONFEDERATE FLAG

More than 150 years after the end of the Civil War, people are still arguing about the Confederate flag. People against the flag say it is an enduring symbol of racism that honors a time in which Black people had no rights and were kept as slaves by white people. To them, it represents inequality, segregation, hatred of Black people, and white nationalism. People who support the use of the flag say it has come to represent the South and its culture and has nothing to do with racism. Many also note they have a right to free speech, which includes flying the Confederate flag.

A CHANGE IN CORPORATE MESSAGING

In the wake of the protests, many of the world's biggest and most iconic brands pledged their support for the Black Lives Matter movement. Some companies, such as Adidas and Nike, had been criticized for hiring mostly white employees while using Black athletes to sell their products. In the wake of Floyd's death, Adidas said it would invest $120 million in Black communities over the next four years, as well as hire Black and Hispanic workers for at least 30 percent of all new positions. Other

Athletes such as basketball star LeBron James have used their sponsorships to promote equality in the United States.

corporate giants made major changes as well. On June 11, Apple increased its spending with Black-owned suppliers as part of a $100 million racial equity and justice initiative. Google's YouTube video service pledged $100 million to fund Black content creators.[5]

In addition to donating money and changing the makeup of their workforces, some companies altered their visual messaging. On June 17, Quaker promised to revamp the name and branding of its popular pancake syrup, Aunt Jemima, which originally featured a Black woman dressed as a minstrel character. "We recognize Aunt Jemima's origins are based on a racial stereotype," said Kristin Kroepfl, vice president and chief marketing officer of Quaker Foods North America. "As we work to make progress toward racial equality through several initiatives, we also must take a hard look at our portfolio of brands and ensure they reflect our values and meet our consumers' expectations."[6]

ANTI-RACIST ENTERTAINMENT AND SPORTS

The impact of Floyd's death was even felt throughout the sports and entertainment industries. The National Football League (NFL) vowed to donate $250 million over the next decade to "end systemic racism." The Washington Redskins football team had long been criticized for having a name that is offensive to many Native Americans. After facing more backlash following Floyd's death, the team announced it would change its name. "This is a good decision for the country—not just Native peoples—since it closes a painful chapter of denigration and disrespect toward Native Americans and other people of color," said Ray Halbritter, Oneida Nation representative and founder of the Change the Mascot campaign.[7]

In the entertainment world, people demanded the publishing industry produce more books by Black authors and writers of color, as well as increase the diversity of their editorial, marketing, publicity, and executive staffs. *Cops*, a TV show that debuted in 1989 and followed real-life police officers on the job, was pulled from

People protested the Washington Redskins mascot years before Floyd's death.

distribution because critics said it glorified police violence. HBO updated the Oscar-winning 1939 film *Gone with the Wind* on its streaming service, adding an introduction that discusses how the film does not accurately represent the awful conditions of slavery. The film also has caricatured depictions of enslaved people and rosy portrayals of the South just prior to the Civil War. "We felt that to keep this title up without an explanation and a denouncement of those depictions would be irresponsible," an HBO Max spokesperson told *Variety*.[8]

ANTI-RACIST READING LISTS

In the aftermath of Floyd's death, media outlets published lists of anti-racist, pro-equality titles about what it's like to be a Black person today. Some people criticized this move as too little, too late. Still, the lists were circulated far and wide.

For example, civil rights lawyer and author Michelle Alexander recommends the following books on these topics: Ibram X. Kendi's *How to Be an Antiracist*, *Stamped from the Beginning*, and *Stamped*, Kendi's young adult book coauthored with Jason Reynolds; Keeanga-Yamahtta Taylor's *From #BlackLivesMatter to Black Liberation*; and Andrea Ritchie's *Invisible No More: Police Violence against Black Women and Women of Color*.

TOUCHING THE WORLD

After Floyd's death on May 25, 2020, many industries were affected. Many people the world over had decided they'd had enough. "Floyd will likely not be the last African American man to die in a case resonant with racial overtones," wrote

Collinson. "His death has not changed the reality of being Black in America—or elsewhere. African American dads will still have to talk to their kids about how to behave around police officers."[9]

"WE NEED JUSTICE FOR GEORGE FLOYD. . . . NO MORE SENSELESS KILLINGS OF HUMAN BEINGS. NO MORE SEEING PEOPLE OF COLOR AS LESS THAN HUMAN. WE CAN NO LONGER LOOK AWAY."[10]

—BEYONCÉ KNOWLES IN A RESPONSE TO GEORGE FLOYD'S DEATH

Still, more people than ever before started to fight for equality under the law, justice for wrongs committed, and freedom not just for white people but all people. With his life and enduring legacy, Floyd touched the world in more ways than he could probably have imagined possible.

Thousands of people came together after Floyd's death to push for justice and change.

ESSENTIAL
FACTS

MAJOR EVENTS

- On May 25, 2020, George Floyd is approached by police under suspicion of using a counterfeit $20 bill. During the incident, police shove him to the ground and hold him there for around eight minutes. He soon dies, sparking worldwide protests for justice and change.

- On May 26, 2020, protests begin in Minneapolis and soon spread throughout the country and across the globe. The four officers involved in the altercation that led to Floyd's death are fired.

- On May 29, 2020, Derek Chauvin, one officer who held Floyd down, is charged with murder. The other three officers are charged five days later for aiding and abetting.

- In the days after Floyd's death, rioters around the world take to the streets at night, burning and looting businesses.

KEY PLAYERS

- Floyd's death sparked protests across the United States and around the world.

- Former police officer Chauvin was caught on camera kneeling on Floyd's neck for around eight minutes. Other officers charged in the Floyd case were Tou Thao, J. Alexander Kueng, and Thomas Lane.

- Philonise Floyd, George Floyd's brother, addressed the United Nations Human Rights Council and asked for help stopping systemic racism in the United States.

- Protesters across the United States took to the streets to demand justice for Floyd and changes to policing.

IMPACT ON SOCIETY

After Floyd's death at the hands of the police, protests erupted around the world. Demonstrators shouted "Black Lives Matter" and called for police reform. Global, national, and local companies and organizations began to revamp their hiring practices to include more people of color. They also did away with branding that contained controversial imagery. What happened to Floyd changed the way people viewed race and equality in the United States and around the world.

QUOTE

"I want to touch the world."

—George Floyd, as recalled by friend Jonathan Veal

GLOSSARY

ABETTING
Encouraging someone to do something wrong, as in a crime.

AUTOPSY
The examination of a body after death to determine the cause of death.

CHOKE HOLD
A general term for a move police use to restrict a person's movement, which usually reduces or prevents either air or blood from passing through the neck.

COUNTERFEIT
Fake.

HOMICIDE
When one person kills another person.

LOOTING
To steal products from a store, often during a riot.

NO-KNOCK WARRANT
Legal approval that allows the police to enter a private residence without announcing their presence.

PREJUDICE
An unfair feeling of dislike for a person or group because of race, sex, or religion.

PROBABLE CAUSE
The legal requirement that law enforcement must have an adequate reason based on facts to arrest someone, search or seize property, or obtain a warrant.

PROVOCATION
An action or speech that makes someone or a group of people angry, usually on purpose.

REPARATIONS
Amends for wrongs that have been done, such as payments for wrongful death when in police custody.

SYSTEMIC
Widespread throughout a whole system, group, or organization.

TEAR GAS
A toxic substance that causes serious irritation to the eyes, sometimes used in riots to force crowds to disperse.

VANDALISM
The illegal destruction of property.

ADDITIONAL
RESOURCES

SELECTED BIBLIOGRAPHY

Baker, Mike, et al. "Three Words, 70 Cases. The Tragic History of 'I Can't Breathe.'" *New York Times*, 29 June 2020, nytimes.com. Accessed 31 July 2020.

Miller, Eric, and Nicholas Pfosi. "Protests, Looting Erupt in Minneapolis over Racially Charged Killing by Police." *Reuters*, 27 May 2020, reuters.com. Accessed 31 July 2020.

Nodjimbadem, Katie. "The Long, Painful History of Police Brutality in the US." *Smithsonian*, 27 July 2017, smithsonianmag.com. Accessed 31 July 2020.

FURTHER READINGS

Edwards, Sue Bradford. *What Are Race and Racism?* Abdo, 2018.

Harris, Duchess, with A.W. Buckey. *Policing in America*. Abdo, 2021.

Harris, Duchess, with Gail Radley. *The Impact of Slavery in America*. Abdo, 2020.

ONLINE RESOURCES

To learn more about policing and inequality, please visit **abdobooklinks.com** or scan this QR code. These links are routinely monitored and updated to provide the most current information available.

MORE INFORMATION

For more information on this subject, contact or visit the following organizations:

American Civil Liberties Union (ACLU)
125 Broad St., Eighteenth Floor
New York, NY 10004
212-549-2500
aclu.org
The ACLU is a nonprofit organization that is dedicated to defending people's constitutional rights on issues of race, police reform, immigration, capital punishment, reproductive rights, free speech, juvenile justice, HIV/AIDS, voting rights, women's rights, LGBTQ rights, and disability rights.

Black Lives Matter
blacklivesmatter.com
Formed in 2013, the Black Lives Matter network works to bring justice, healing, and freedom to Black people across the globe. It works with activists, grassroots organizers, journalists, and experts on issues concerning racial injustice, police brutality, criminal justice reform, Black immigration, economic injustice, LGBTQ rights, environmental injustice, access to health care, access to quality education, and voting rights.

SOURCE NOTES

CHAPTER 1. "I CAN'T BREATHE"

1. Evan Hill et al. "How George Floyd Was Killed in Police Custody." *New York Times*, 31 May 2020, nytimes.com. Accessed 1 Oct. 2020.

2. "Transcript." *New York Times*, 7 July 2020, int.nyt.com. Accessed 1 Oct. 2020.

3. "Transcript."

4. "Transcript."

5. "Ex-Officer Derek Chauvin the Subject of at Least 17 Complaints." *KCRG*, 4 June 2020, kcrg.com. Accessed 1 Oct. 2020.

6. "Transcript."

7. Nicholas Bogel-Burroughs. "8 Minutes, 46 Seconds Became a Symbol in George Floyd's Death. The Exact Time Is Less Clear." *New York Times*, 18 June 2020, nytimes.com. Accessed 1 Oct. 2020.

8. "Transcript."

9. Neil MacFarquhar. "In George Floyd's Death, a Police Technique Results in a Too-Familiar Tragedy." *New York Times*, 29 May 2020, nytimes.com. Accessed 1 Oct. 2020.

10. Vanessa Romo. "County Officials Rule George Floyd Death Was a Homicide." *NPR*, 1 June 2020, npr.org. Accessed 6 Oct. 2020.

11. Joshua Nevett. "George Floyd: The Personal Cost of Filming Police Brutality." *BBC*, 11 June 2020, bbc.com. Accessed 1 Oct. 2020.

12. Mike Baker et al. "Three Words. 70 Cases. The Tragic History of 'I Can't Breathe.'" *New York Times*, 29 June 2020, nytimes.com. Accessed 1 Oct. 2020.

13. "When Byron Williams Died Saying 'I Can't Breathe,' Few Protested. Now His Family Is Fighting for Justice." *NBC Philadelphia*, 18 June 2020, nbcphiladelphia.com. Accessed 1 Oct. 2020.

CHAPTER 2. WHO WAS GEORGE FLOYD?

1. Manny Fernandez and Audra D. S. Burch. "George Floyd, from 'I Want to Touch the World' to 'I Can't Breathe.'" *New York Times*, 29 July 2020, nytimes.com. Accessed 1 Oct. 2020.

2. Luis Andres Henao et al. "A Long Look at the Complicated Life of George Floyd." *Chicago Tribune*, 11 June 2020, chicagotribune.com. Accessed 1 Oct. 2020.

3. Fernandez and Burch, "George Floyd, from 'I Want to Touch the World' to 'I Can't Breathe.'"

4. Henao et al., "A Long Look at the Complicated Life of George Floyd."

5. David Greene. "Houston's Hip-Hop Scene Remembers George Floyd." *NPR*, 10 June 2020, npr.org. Accessed 1 Oct. 2020.

6. Henao et al., "A Long Look at the Complicated Life of George Floyd."

7. Kerri Miller and Marcheta Fornoff. "Life after Prison: The 'Sentence Never Ends.'" *MPR News*, 8 Mar. 2017, mprnews.org. Accessed 1 Oct. 2020.

8. Fionnuala O'Leary. "George Floyd's Grieving Girlfriend Courtney Ross Reveals Her Final Words to Him Were 'I Love You.'" *US Sun*, 5 June 2020, the-sun.com. Accessed 1 Oct. 2020.

9. Nurith Aizenman. "COVID-19 Deaths Top 1 Million Worldwide. How These 5 Nations Are Driving the Pandemic." *NPR*, 28 Sept. 2020, npr.org. Accessed 1 Oct. 2020.

CHAPTER 3. THE HISTORY OF POLICE BRUTALITY

1. Katie Nodjimbadem. "The Long, Painful History of Police Brutality in the US." *Smithsonian*, 27 July 2017, smithsonianmag.com. Accessed 1 Oct. 2020.

2. Nodjimbadem, "The Long, Painful History of Police Brutality in the US."

3. Wenei Philimon. "Not Just George Floyd: Police Departments Have 400-Year History of Racism." *USA Today*, 7 June 2020, usatoday.com. Accessed 1 Oct. 2020.

4. Sarah Brady Siff. "Policing the Police: A Civil Rights Story." *Origins*, May 2016, origins.osu.edu. Accessed 1 Oct. 2020.

5. Isabel Wilkerson. "The Long-Lasting Legacy of the Great Migration." *Smithsonian*, Sept. 2016, smithsonianmag.com. Accessed 1 Oct. 2020.

6. "The Great Migration." *WTTW*, n.d., wttw.com. Accessed 1 Oct. 2020.

7. Nodjimbadem, "The Long, Painful History of Police Brutality in the US."

8. Olivia B. Waxman. "'It Just Goes On and On': How the Race Riots of 1919's 'Red Summer' Helped Shape a Century of American History." *Time*, 29 July 2019, time.com. Accessed 6 Oct. 2020.

9. Wilkerson, "The Long-Lasting Legacy of the Great Migration."

10. Philimon, "Not Just George Floyd."

11. Tragina Quarks Emeka. "Detroit Riot of 1967." *Britannica*, 16 July 2020, britannica.com. Accessed 1 Oct. 2020.

12. "Anti-Brutality Campaigns." *Britannica*, n.d., britannica.com. Accessed 1 Oct. 2020.

13. "Fatal Force." *Washington Post*, 28 Sept. 2020, washingtonpost.com. Accessed 1 Oct. 2020.

14. Nodjimbadem, "The Long, Painful History of Police Brutality in the US."

CHAPTER 4. PROTESTS AND RIOTS IN MINNEAPOLIS

1. Mark Morales et al. "Louisville Agrees to Pay Breonna Taylor's Family $12 Million and Enact Police Reforms in Historic Settlement." *CNN*, 15 Sept. 2020, cnn.com. Accessed 1 Oct. 2020.

2. "Breonna Taylor: Timeline of Black Deaths Caused by Police." *BBC*, 23 Sept. 2020, bbc.com. Accessed 1 Oct. 2020.

3. Kimberly Kindy et al. "Fatal Police Shootings in 2015 Approaching 400 Nationwide." *Washington Post*, 30 May 2015, washingtonpost.com. Accessed 6 Oct. 2020.

4. Audra D. S. Burch and John Eligon. "Bystander Videos of George Floyd and Others Are Policing the Police." *New York Times*, 26 May 2020, nytimes.com. Accessed 1 Oct. 2020.

5. Natalie Colarossi. "Photos Show Thousands of Protesters Demanding Justice in Minneapolis after Police Killed George Floyd." *Insider*, 27 May 2020, insider.com. Accessed 1 Oct. 2020.

6. Burch and Eligon, "Bystander Videos of George Floyd and Others Are Policing the Police."

7. Alex Hagan. "38th and Chicago Could Turn into Permanent George Floyd Memorial." *Kare 11*, 15 June 2020, kare11.com. Accessed 1 Oct. 2020.

8. Ryan Faircloth et al. "Looting and Flames Erupt in Minneapolis Amid Growing Protests over George Floyd's Death." *Star Tribune*, 28 May 2020, startribune.com. Accessed 1 Oct. 2020.

9. Faircloth et al., "Looting and Flames Erupt in Minneapolis."

10. Tony Zaccardi. "I've Had to Paint 'Black Owned Business' on My Minneapolis Bar during the Riots." *Newsweek*, 29 May 2020, newsweek.com. Accessed 1 Oct. 2020.

11. Nina Strochlic. "'We're Hurting, We're Hurting'—Grief and Outrage Converge in Minneapolis." *National Geographic*, 30 May 2020, nationalgeographic.com. Accessed 1 Oct. 2020.

12. Matt Furber et al. "Minneapolis Police, Long Accused of Racism, Face Wrath of Wounded City." *New York Times*, 27 May 2020, nytimes.com. Accessed 1 Oct. 2020.

CHAPTER 5. A NATION DIVIDED

1. Neil MacFarquhar. "Ex-Officer Charged in Death of George Floyd in Minneapolis." *New York Times*, 29 June 2020, nytimes.com. Accessed 1 Oct. 2020.

2. Sarah Mervosh and Nicholas Bogel-Burroughs. "Why Derek Chauvin Was Charged with Third-Degree Murder." *New York Times*, 29 May 2020, nytimes.com. Accessed 1 Oct. 2020.

3. Tyler J. Davis et al. "'No Justice, No Peace': Protesters Breach Minneapolis Police Precinct, Set Fires in the Wake of George Floyd's Death." *MSN*, 29 May 2020, msn.com. Accessed 1 Oct. 2020.

4. Maggie Haberman and Alexander Burns. "Trump's Looting and 'Shooting' Remarks Escalate Crisis in Minneapolis." *New York Times*, 1 June 2020, nytimes.com. Accessed 1 Oct. 2020.

5. Mervosh and Bogel-Burroughs, "Why Derek Chauvin Was Charged with Third-Degree Murder."

6. Maanvi Singh and Nina Lakhani. "George Floyd Killing: Peaceful Protests Sweep America As Calls for Racial Justice Reach New Heights." *Guardian*, 7 June 2020, theguardian.com. Accessed 1 Oct. 2020.

SOURCE NOTES
CONTINUED

7. Edgar Sandoval. "Protests Flare in Brooklyn over Floyd Death As de Blasio Appeals for Calm." *New York Times*, 30 May 2020, nytimes.com. Accessed 1 Oct. 2020.

8. Sandoval, "Protests Flare in Brooklyn over Floyd Death As de Blasio Appeals for Calm."

9. Singh and Lakhani, "George Floyd Killing."

10. Singh and Lakhani, "George Floyd Killing."

11. Kevin Liptak et al. "60 Minutes of Mayhem: How Aggressive Politics and Policing Turned a Peaceful Protest into a Violent Confrontation." *CNN*, 2 June 2020, cnn.com. Accessed 1 Oct. 2020.

12. Dalton Bennett et al. "The Crackdown before Trump's Photo Op." *Washington Post*, 8 June 2020, washingtonpost.com. Accessed 1 Oct. 2020.

13. Kim Barker and Caitlin Dickerson. "March Peacefully or 'Take the Streets'? Protesters Debate What Comes Next." *New York Times*, 2 June 2020, nytimes.com. Accessed 1 Oct. 2020.

14. Olga Khazan. "Why People Loot." *Atlantic*, 2 June 2020, theatlantic.com. Accessed 1 Oct. 2020.

15. Khazan, "Why People Loot."

16. "Stephanie Wilford of Minneapolis, Minnesota, Unrest in the Twin Cities, the Aftermath." *YouTube*, 30 May 2020, youtube.com. Accessed 1 Oct. 2020.

17. Shawn Hubler and Julie Bosman. "A Crisis That Began with an Image of Police Violence Keeps Providing More." *New York Times*, 8 July 2020, nytimes.com. Accessed 1 Oct. 2020.

18. Eric Levenson et al. "The Rev. Al Sharpton Remembers George Floyd As an 'Ordinary Brother' Who Changed the World." *CNN*, 9 June 2020, cnn.com. Accessed 1 Oct. 2020.

CHAPTER 6. GLOBAL SUPPORT

1. Colin Dwyer. "George Floyd's Brother to UN Human Rights Council: 'I Am Asking You to Help Us.'" *NPR*, 17 June 2020, npr.org. Accessed 1 Oct. 2020.

2. NBC News. "George Floyd's Brother to UN: 'I Am Asking You to Help Us, Black People in America.'" *YouTube*, 17 June 2020, youtube.com. Accessed 1 Oct. 2020.

3. Dwyer, "George Floyd's Brother to UN Human Rights Council: 'I Am Asking You to Help Us.'"

4. Damien Cave et al. "Huge Crowds around the Globe March in Solidarity against Police Brutality." *New York Times*, 6 June 2020, nytimes.com. Accessed 1 Oct. 2020.

5. Brian Naylor and Kelsey Snell. "George Floyd's Brother Tells Lawmakers Justice Has to Be Served." *NPR*, 10 June 2020, npr.org. Accessed 1 Oct. 2020.

6. Lauren Collins. "Assa Traoré and the Fight for Black Lives in France." *New Yorker*, 18 June 2020, newyorker.com. Accessed 1 Oct. 2020.

7. "Black Lives Matter: Where Does 'Taking a Knee' Come From?" *BBC*, 18 June 2020, bbc.com. Accessed 1 Oct. 2020.

8. Juliet Macur. "Colin Kaepernick's Anthem Protest Leaves the NFL Necessarily Uneasy." *New York Times*, 7 Sept. 2016, nytimes.com. Accessed 1 Oct. 2020.

9. "Roger Goodell: 'Wish We Had Listened Earlier' to What Colin Kaepernick Was Protesting." *ESPN*, 23 Aug. 2020, espn.com. Accessed 6 Oct. 2020.

10. Suyin Haynes. "As Protesters Shine a Spotlight on Racial Injustice in America, the Reckoning Is Going Global." *Time*, 11 June 2020, time.com. Accessed 1 Oct. 2020.

11. Nana Akufo-Addo. "#GeorgeFloyd #JusticeForGeorgeFloyd." *Twitter*, 1 June 2020, twitter.com. Accessed 1 Oct. 2020.

12. Haynes, "As Protesters Shine a Spotlight on Racial Injustice in America."

13. Richard A. Oppel Jr. et al. "The Fullest Look Yet at the Racial Inequity of Coronavirus." *New York Times*, 5 July 2020, nytimes.com. Accessed 1 Oct. 2020.

14. Jen Kirby. "'Black Lives Matter' Has Become a Global Rallying Cry against Racism and Police Brutality." *Vox*, 12 June 2020, vox.com. Accessed 1 Oct. 2020.

15. Ben Makori and Hannah McKay. "Rhodes Must Fall—Oxford Protesters Target Statue of Colonialist." *Reuters*, 9 June 2020, reuters.com. Accessed 1 Oct. 2020.

16. "About." *Black Lives Matter*, n.d., blacklivesmatter.com. Accessed 1 Oct. 2020.

CHAPTER 7. A CALL FOR REFORM

1. Michael Barbaro. "A Conversation with a Police Union Leader." *New York Times*, 29 June 2020, nytimes.com. Accessed 1 Oct. 2020.

2. Vera Bergengruen and Tessa Berenson. "'It Was a Tinderbox.' How George Floyd's Killing Highlighted America's Police Reform Failures." *Time*, 4 June 2020, time.com. Accessed 1 Oct. 2020.

3. Barbaro, "A Conversation with a Police Union Leader."

4. Barbaro, "A Conversation with a Police Union Leader."

5. Noam Scheiber et al. "How Police Unions Became Such Powerful Opponents to Reform Efforts." *New York Times*, 6 June 2020, nytimes.com. Accessed 1 Oct. 2020.

6. Reade Levinson. "Across the US, Police Contracts Shield Officers from Scrutiny and Discipline." *Reuters*, 13 Jan. 2017, reuters.com. Accessed 1 Oct. 2020.

7. Levinson, "Across the US, Police Contracts Shield Officers from Scrutiny and Discipline."

8. Steven Greenhouse. "How Police Unions Enable and Conceal Abuses of Power." *New Yorker*, 18 June 2020, newyorker.com. Accessed 1 Oct. 2020.

9. Hailey Fuchs. "Qualified Immunity Protection for Police Emerges As Flash Point Amid Protests." *New York Times*, 23 June 2020, nytimes.com. Accessed 1 Oct. 2020.

10. Zachary Fagenson. "Defund the Police: What It Means and Why It's Important." *Complex*, 15 June 2020, complex.com. Accessed 1 Oct. 2020.

11. Jason C. Johnson and James A. Gagliano. "Defunding the Police Isn't the Answer." *CNN*, 9 June 2020, cnn.com. Accessed 1 Oct. 2020.

12. Fagenson, "Defund the Police."

13. Brady Dennis et al. "Dallas Police Chief Says 'We're Asking Cops to Do Too Much in This Country.'" *Washington Post*, 11 July 2016, washingtonpost.com. Accessed 1 Oct. 2020.

14. Katherine Landergan. "A City That Really Did Abolish the Police." *Politico*, 12 June 2020, politico.com. Accessed 1 Oct. 2020.

CHAPTER 8. GEORGE FLOYD'S LEGACY

1. Stephen Collinson. "As George Floyd Is Laid to Rest, His Legacy Reverberates across the Globe." *CNN*, 10 June 2020, cnn.com. Accessed 1 Oct. 2020.

2. "Four Numbers That Explain the Impact of George Floyd." *BBC*, 25 June 2020, bbc.com. Accessed 1 Oct. 2020.

3. Amita Kelly and Brian Naylor. "Trump, Hailing Law Enforcement, Signs Executive Order Calling for Police Reform." *NPR*, 16 June 2020, npr.org. Accessed 1 Oct. 2020.

4. Chandelis Duster and Paul LeBlanc. "Mississippi Governor Signs Bill to Retire Flag with Confederate Emblem." *CNN*, 30 June 2020, cnn.com. Accessed 1 Oct. 2020.

5. "Factbox: What Changes Are Companies Making in Response to George Floyd Protests?" *Reuters*, 16 June 2020, reuters.com. Accessed 1 Oct. 2020.

6. Ben Kesslen. "Aunt Jemima Brand to Change Name, Remove Image That Quaker Says Is 'Based on a Racial Stereotype.'" *NBC News*, 17 June 2020, nbcnews.com. Accessed 1 Oct. 2020.

7. "Washington Redskins to Drop Controversial Team Name Following Review." *BBC*, 13 July 2020, bbc.com. Accessed 1 Oct. 2020.

8. Lisa Richwine. "'Gone with the Wind,' 'Cops' Pulled As Pop Culture Reckons with Racism." *Reuters*, 10 June 2020, reuters.com. Accessed 1 Oct. 2020.

9. Collinson, "As George Floyd Is Laid to Rest, His Legacy Reverberates across the Globe."

10. Chloe Melas. "Beyoncé Demands Justice for George Floyd." *CNN*, 1 June 2020, cnn.com. Accessed 1 Oct. 2020.

INDEX

Arbery, Ahmaud, 50–51
Arradondo, Medaria, 42

Black Lives Matter (BLM), 57, 67, 69,
  73, 74–75, 87, 93–94
branding, 94–96
Brown, Michael, 41, 75, 76

Chauvin, Derek, 4, 7–11, 43, 52, 54,
  58, 67
choke hold, 10, 12, 42, 86, 92–93
civil rights movement, 26, 33
Civil War, 28, 93–94, 98
Clark, Stephon, 75
complaints, 7, 81–82, 88
Congress, 86
Constitution, 31
COVID-19, 21–23, 38, 43, 70, 72
Crump, Ben, 40
Cup Foods, 4, 11
curfew, 55, 58

defunding police, 57, 79, 81, 87
discrimination, 33, 71, 78
diversity, 32, 97
drugs, 11, 18, 20, 38, 40, 88–89

Equal Justice Initiative, 31
excessive force, 7, 27, 86, 88

Federal Bureau of Investigation (FBI),
  42, 87
flash grenades, 45, 57
Floyd, Philonise, 64, 66–67
Floyd, Terrence, 58
Fountain of Praise Church, 62
Frazier, Darnella, 8, 11
Freeman, Mike, 43
Frey, Jacob, 43, 46, 54–55

Garner, Eric, 12–13
Gray, Freddie, 60, 76, 78
Great Migration, 28, 32

Holmes, Malcolm D., 37
homicide, 11, 58
Human Rights Council, 64, 66

immigrants, 26

Jack Yates High School, 14, 16
Johnson, Lyndon B., 35

Kaepernick, Colin, 69
King, Rodney, 35
Kueng, J. Alexander, 4, 6-7, 58

Lane, Thomas, 4, 6-7, 58
lawsuit, 13, 40
looting, 45-46, 54, 58, 60
lynching, 31, 67, 86

manslaughter, 52, 54, 58
Martin, Trayvon, 74
Mbegbu, Balantine, 12
Mississippi state flag, 93-94
Moore, Leonard, 26, 31-32
mural, 45
murder, 26, 51, 52, 54, 58, 64, 93

National Advisory Commission on
    Civil Disorders, 35
National Football League (NFL), 69,
    96
National Guard, 48, 54
National Museum of African
    American History and Culture, 24
night watchmen, 27
no-knock warrant, 38

paramedics, 9, 11
pepper spray, 56, 59
police brutality, 11, 23, 24, 26-27,
    30, 37, 63, 66-67, 86, 93
police reform, 40, 78, 81, 83, 86-87,
    89, 92
police unions, 81-83, 88
prejudice, 26, 30-31, 71, 80
prison, 10 20, 58

qualified immunity, 81, 83-86

Red Summer, 31
Resurrection Houston, 19
Rice, Tamir, 41
riots, 31, 33-37, 46-47, 54-55, 57,
    58-60, 70
rubber bullets, 45, 57, 61

segregation, 33, 94
Sharpton, Al, 63
social media, 8, 11, 19, 40, 54, 78
South Africa National Defense Force,
    70
South Florida Community College, 17
state of emergency, 48
Sterling, Alton, 41

Taylor, Breonna, 38, 40, 42, 56
tear gas, 33, 45, 56-57
Thao, Tou, 4, 7, 58
Trump, Donald, 54, 57, 92-93

vandalism, 58, 60, 68, 75
Veal, Jonathan, 14, 16

Walz, Tim, 48
Wilford, Stephanie, 60
Williams, Byron, 12
World Health Organization, 22
World War I, 31
World War II, 31

ABOUT THE
AUTHORS

DUCHESS HARRIS, JD, PhD

Dr. Harris is a professor of American Studies and Political Science at Macalester College and curator of the Duchess Harris Collection of ABDO books. She is also the coauthor of the collection, which features popular titles such as *Hidden Human Computers: The Black Women of NASA* and series including Freedom's Promise and Race and American Law. In addition, Dr. Harris hosts the Freedom's Promise podcast with her son.

Before working with ABDO, Dr. Harris authored several other books on the topics of race, culture, and American history. She served as an associate editor for *Litigation News*, the American Bar Association Section of Litigation's quarterly flagship publication, and was the first editor in chief of *Law Raza*, an interactive online journal covering race and the law, published at William Mitchell College of Law. She has earned a BA in History from the University of Pennsylvania, a PhD in American Studies from the University of Minnesota, and a JD from William Mitchell College of Law.

ALEXIS BURLING

Alexis Burling has written dozens of articles and books for young readers on a variety of topics including current events, famous people, nutrition and fitness, careers and money management, relationships, and cooking. She is also a book critic with reviews of both adult and young adult books, author interviews, and other industry-related articles published in the *New York Times*, *Washington Post*, *San Francisco Chronicle*, and more. Burling lives with her husband in Portland, Oregon, where protesters marched daily for months in honor of George Floyd and Black Lives Matter.